Breath by Breath

Breath by Breath

The Liberating Practice
of Insight Liberation

Larry Rosenberg
with David Guy

Foreword by
Jon Kabat-Zinn

Shambhala
Boston & London
1998

Shambhala Publications, Inc.
Horticultural Hall
300 Massachusetts Avenue
Boston, MA 02115
http://www.shambhala.com

9 8 7 6 5 4 3 2 1

First Edition
Printed in the United States of America
⊗ This edition is printed on acid-free paper that meets the
American National Standards Institute Z39.48 Standard.
Distributed in the United States by Random House, Inc.,
and in Canada by Random House of Canada Ltd

Library of Congress Cataloging-in-Publication Data
Rosenberg, Larry.
        Breath by breath: the liberating practice of insight
    meditation/Larry Rosenberg; with David Guy;
    foreword by Jon Kabat-Zinn.—1st ed.
        p.   cm.
    ISBN 1-57062-335-X (cloth: alk. paper)
        1. Meditation.   2. Ānāpānasmṛti.
    I. Guy, David.   II. Title.
    BL627.R67   1998   97-29041
    291.4′35—dc21   CIP

To my beloved parents, Anna and Nathan Rosenberg.
They gave me everything they had.

Contents

Foreword   ix

Acknowledgments   xiii

A Note on Terminology   xvii

Introduction: Finding My Way   1

1. Breathing with the Body   10

2. Breathing with Feelings   51

3. Breathing with the Mind   80

4. Breathing with Wisdom   112

5. The Condensed Method: Breathing
   with the Way Things Are   149

6. Breathing with Daily Life   159

7. Breathing into Silence   183

Appendix: The Anapanasati Sutra   198

Glossary   209

Bibliography   213

Resources   215

Foreword

This book is the product of an ongoing spiritual odyssey on the part of the author that I have had the privilege to observe and, from time to time, share in over the more than thirty years that he and I have been what we fondly refer to as "Dharma brothers." It is a journey of exploration that has never deviated—even in the most difficult and painful of times—from the target that Larry Rosenberg set for himself early on: the deepest personal encounter with the heart of wisdom practice, whatever the source; the deepest drinking in of what such practices had to offer; and the uncompromising embodiment of that understanding in the domain of ordinary living in the secular world. Now, in this touching and poignant book, he speaks with authority, passion, and his own inimitable brand of Brooklyn Jewish humor, on the practice of meditation at its most basic and its most exquisite.

Larry has chosen to structure his teachings here based on the *Anapanasati Sutra*, a text that has been commented upon time and time again throughout history in Buddhist circles, much as the Torah has occasioned generations of commentary and insight in the Jewish tradition. This text constitutes the basic meditative instructions of the Buddha, and so serves as a fundamental vehicle for gaining insight into the core teachings of Buddhism. As with all great classical texts, each teacher's interpretation, whether primarily scholarly or practical, is colored by his or her unique perspective and voice. Each individual who tackles the task tends to bring out different facets of the basic message. In recent years, Buddhadasa Bhikkhu (*Mindfulness with Breathing*) and Thich Nhat Hanh (*Breathe, You Are Alive*) have contributed important interpretations of this sutra. Now Larry, who has studied with both of these teachers, as he himself explains, brings his own remarkable gifts to the task of using the teachings of the *Anapanasati Sutra* to make the practice of insight meditation come alive for the reader/practitioner.

Breath by Breath is more than one more in a long line of venerable and valuable commentaries on this text. Larry's treatment illuminates the sutra's essence and its practical utility in a wholly contemporary Western idiom, making it tangible, compelling, and immediately relevant for anybody who is seriously interested in developing a personal meditation practice.

Here the four-by-fourfold framework of the sutra itself serves as a loom on which the author skillfully weaves, in front of the reader's very eyes, the tapestry of mindfulness meditation practice in all its simplicity, fullness, and depth. When the tapestry is complete, the loom of the sutra has fulfilled its purpose. What we are left with is an understanding of the practice in its exquisite simplicity, its precisely defined detail, and its transformative power, as well as a way to keep it vital and fresh through our own growing passion and appreciation for the path of inquiry it invites us to explore.

The ability to evoke an impact of such magnitude, whether in speech or in writing, is a sign of a great teacher. The depth of Larry's understanding is apparent in his approach to the breath as a complete vehicle for the cultivation of mindfulness, compassion, and wisdom. His clarity is complemented by his commitment to keep things simple and demystified, and by his easy-going and delightful sense of humor. All shine through on virtually every page of this book.

Larry is not kidding around, simple and humorous as this book may appear to be in places. The cultivation of mindfulness is ultimately a matter of life and death, not in a scary way, but in the sense that we are always at risk, in every moment, for missing what is deepest and richest in our lives, the texture of the tapestry itself. We might say (every pun intended) that the richness lies right beneath our noses in any and every moment. This book is an invitation to recognize that richness through our own daily inner work on ourselves, culminating in an uncompromising and accurate intimacy with our minds, our bodies, and our breathing, guided by the sutra, a precious intimacy that can serve as a door to awakening and freedom.

Meditation is a lifetime's work. It usually deepens as we arrive incrementally at degrees of understanding—we often think we understand some aspect of practice or life; then, after more practice, it is not uncommon to find our understanding to be more encompassing and deeper, or perhaps totally different from what it was before. *The Sutra on the Full Awareness of Breathing*, reflecting the meditation practice itself, is truly limitless in its implications and importance. For this reason, *Breath by Breath* merits reading over and over again in its entirety, as well as dipping into here and there frequently, as both a reminder and a guide to practice.

It is commonly said that the ancient peoples of the north have many words to describe the subtleties of what we refer to merely as "snow," and that those of the forest have hundreds of words for shades of green. Anybody who meditates knows that the same might be said of the breath. Each breath moment is its own universe. In meditation, we come to know something about this terrain in ways that open doors, that bring us back to our senses, that refine our hearts, that help us understand what it means to be human, what it means to be whole, right here, right now.

No two breaths are the same; no two moments are the same. Each one is our life. Each one is infinitely deep and complete in itself. The challenge here is to embody and live this awareness, to work with the automatic habits of mind that would turn us into automatons and betray our genius, to walk our own path, as Larry is continually encouraging the reader to do, to find our own way, breath by breath, to taste silence and discover liberation within each and any breath.

This book will be of great utility, reassurance, and inspiration for all those wishing to embark on or resurrect a formal path of meditation practice, or for those who wish to refine and deepen their practice, or to hear once again, in its timeless beauty and its particular unique incarnation here through the voice of a seasoned and wonderful teacher—a Dharma lion in a lineage of wonderful teachers and Dharma lions, each unique, going back to the Buddha—the universal wisdom of the Dharma.

Jon Kabat-Zinn
August 1997

Acknowledgments

Experiencing and expressing gratitude is a vital aspect of Dharma practice. None of us can live alone: we need food, clothing, medicine, shelter, and, of course, the support of our friends. Everything depends on everything else. This book is no exception. So much help turned up! Here is a short list of some who have helped:

J. Krishnamurti, Vimala Thakar, and Zen Master Seung Sahn were my first spiritual teachers. They did not directly contribute to this book, but the profound impact of their teachings on my life effects everything I do. Krishnaji continues to inspire and guide me from the grave, Vimalaji from Mount Abu, India, and Seung Sahn from all over the world.

Vimalo Kulbarz, in his inimitable erudite and humorous manner, introduced me to the Buddha's teaching on anapanasati. What a difference it has made!

In writing this commentary, I have benefited from the immense contributions to Dharma and *anapanasati* made by my teachers Ajahn Buddhadasa and Thich Nhat Hanh. Their contribution to my understanding is present throughout this work. I am deeply grateful for all that they have given me.

Santikaro Bhikkhu generously gave me access to many tapes and unpublished materials of Ajahn Buddhadasa on the *Anapanasati Sutra*. Over the years he has been extremely helpful in clarifying these teachings.

Thanissaro Bhikkhu, through his writing and generous personal sharing, has given me access to another vital stream of breath meditation teaching and practice, the lineage of Ajahn Lee of Thailand. His incisive critical reading of this work in manuscript form was invaluable to me. Many of his suggestions have been incorporated into the final text.

Bhante Gunaratana heard a two-hour oral presentation of the essence of what has become this book. He was very encouraging. His enthusiasm has been more important to me that he will ever know.

Dainin Katagiri Roshi and Zen Master George Bowman, in many discussions, helped deepen my understanding of the Zen perspective on posture, breathing, and "just sitting," a practice with many parallels in anapanasati.

Jon Kabat-Zinn, Narayan Liebenson-Grady, and Corrado Pensa commented on the entire manuscript, substantially enhancing its quality. Narayan, Corrado, Sarah Doering, and Michael Liebenson-Grady, my teaching comrades at the Cambridge Insight Meditation Center (CIMC), Cambridge, Massachusetts, and the Insight Meditation Society (IMS), Barre, Massachusetts, have also been wonderful sources of learning for me over the years. My understanding of vipassana meditation and the process of communicating these understandings continues to be refined in association with these devoted servants of the Dharma. I have also appreciated their patience with my ebullience during the first few years of my teaching anapanasati. I was a bit much, yet they good-naturedly put up with my obsession.

Many of the yogis at the CIMC and the IMS asked challenging questions and gave candid reports on their experiences of the *Anapanasati Sutra* in action. Much of what I learned from these exchanges is part of this book.

This book is based on transcripts of more than forty talks given over a three-year period at CIMC, IMS, and the Barre Center for Buddhist Studies. I would periodically look at this mountain of printed material and immediately find something else to do. Many people helped rescue me from this predicament, including Dorothea Bowen, Ruth Nelson, and Tom Jackson, each of whom devoted a great deal of time, effort, and editorial skill to an early and very helpful version of the text.

David Guy was able to perform surgery on this mass of material with the precision of a brain surgeon. He also subordinated his own literary voice in order to assist me in preserving the spirit and flavor of the original talks. Many meditators at the CIMC generously gave time to the accurate transcription of each recorded talk.

Dave O'Neal, my editor at Shambhala Publications, combined great competence with an unassuming and relaxed approach to the discipline needed to turn lots of words into a book. He was a joy to work with.

Jacalyn Bennett for many years provided warm and unwavering encouragement to me to put these oral teachings into written form, and also made it possible by generously providing the financial support needed to bring the project to fruition.

Andrew Hier provided the gift of a personal computer—just when I needed it.

Colette Bourassa and Pash Voynow, Director and Assistant Director of CIMC, patiently and lovingly helped in many ways to bring the publication of this book to its consummation.

Just when it seemed like this book would wander forever in search of a title, Sharon Salzberg called. She and Erik McCord came up with *Breath by Breath*, a phrase I have used thousands of times in teaching anapanasati in the past few years.

My wife, Galina, was masterful in her ability to know when to encourage me to get back to the computer, and when to turn it off and relax. I am very appreciative of her loving support and understanding during every phase of the intense and demanding period of time needed for writing.

May any merit arising from this book be directed to Nathan Rosenberg and Mary Bennett to help them on their spiritual journeys. They died before this work was completed.

Just before I left his monastery in Thailand, I asked Ajahn Buddhadasa for any advice he might have regarding the teaching of Dharma in the West. He replied that it was important to be both very conservative and very radical: the core of the Buddha's teaching is precious and needs to be conserved; however, to convey the teachings in this new culture, I would have to be somewhat radical. The challenge is to present these teachings and practices in a manner that is appropriate for Westerners—but without distorting the essence of what the Buddha had in mind. Ajahn Buddhadasa's advice has been my compass and source of inspiration in writing this book. I sincerely hope my response to such intelligent guidance is adequate.

A Note on Terminology

The anapanasati teachings are in the Pali language, and Pali words used in the text are defined where they are used and in the glossary. But a few Mahayana Sanskrit words have become so familiar to readers of Buddhist books in the English language that we have used the Sanskrit for those words rather than the Pali. We therefore refer to a *sutra* rather than a *sutta*, to the *Dharma* rather than the *Dhamma*, and to *nirvana* rather than *nibbana*.

The Pali word *bhikkhu* appears often in the actual text of the *Anapanasati Sutra*. It is usually translated as "monk," with an acknowledgment that this term applies to any serious meditator— male or female, monk or layperson. Because most of the readers of this text will probably be laypeople, we have used the words meditator and practitioner when referring to students of the sutra.

The translation of the *Anapanasati Sutra* that we use is derived primarily from the translation of Thanissaro Bhikku. I have made a number of modifications in his terminology. These changes are my responsibility.

Breath by Breath

Introduction
Finding My Way

Every student's practice is peculiarly his or her own and comes together in its own way. My practice has unfolded over many years, and it focuses on a particular discourse of the Buddha. But it was some time before I saw the real value of this teaching.

My first teachers were from India, J. Krishnamurti and Vimala Thaker. They were nonsectarian and placed a strong emphasis on maintaining awareness at all times. By the early 1970s I had studied meditation for a number of years, including four years with Vedanta master Swami Chinmayanda. I had worked with the Korean Zen master Seung Sahn for five years and had lived in that country for a year. More recently I had studied Soto Zen with the Japanese master Katagiri Roshi. Gradually I came to see that the Theravada tradition of vipassana meditation was a better match for me. All of these practices are closely related, of course, and can enrich one another.

I was practicing at one of this country's prominent centers of vipassana meditation, the Insight Meditation Society in Barre, Massachusetts, when I encountered a monk named Bhikkhu Vimalo, a German national who had studied for twenty years in Burma, Thailand, and India.

At that point my practice was *samatha/vipassana*; I focused on the breathing in order to calm the mind, then—dropping the breath as an object—opened the attention to a wider focus, noticing the arising and passing away of whatever aspect of body or mind presented itself most vividly. Bhikkhu Vimalo argued that I was seriously limiting my work with the breath, that in fact the breath could take me all the way to the deepest realizations.

He told me of a particular sutra of the Buddha's, the *Anapanasati Sutra*, which outlined how the awareness of breathing could be used systematically to embrace both samatha and vipassana. I was impressed by what Bhikku Vimalo told me and eventually led some retreats with him, but it would be years before I was fully convinced of the importance of breath awareness teaching as a complete practice.

My conversion came during an intense two-hour meeting with the great Thai teacher Ajahn Buddhadasa, an encounter that had a profound impact on my practice and changed my teaching forever. Buddhadasa was nearly eighty when I saw him, and not particularly well, but tireless in his teaching. He often taught informally, sitting in front of his hut in the forest with students— and wild chickens, and a dog—gathered around him. He was convinced that the *Anapanasati Sutra* was a key document for practice and an ideal vehicle for teaching. He took me through the entire sutra step-by-step, in a detailed and painstaking way, part lecture, part meditation instruction. By the time he had finished, I was exhausted and soaking wet. It was one of the most powerful periods of learning I have ever experienced.

To summarize very briefly: the *Anapanasati Sutra* is composed of sixteen contemplations, which divide rather neatly into four sets of four. The first four contemplations concern the awareness of breathing as it manifests in the body. The next four focus on feelings—not what we mean by that word in our culture, but everything that we perceive by means of our sense organs. The third set of four focuses on the mind, the mental formations and emotions that we concoct when we add ideas to our feelings. And the last four move on to pure vipassana, seeing into the lawfulness underlying all phenomena. Basic to all of these contemplations is the breath, which is used in them as an anchor, a reminder, to keep the practitioner in the present moment.

Buddhadasa's approach was rational and systematic but also beautifully timed to open me up emotionally. He knew something of my history, and I had told him of my particular interest in the Zen concept of emptiness. When we got to the thirteenth contemplation—which concerns impermanence, and where real vipassana begins—he said that anapanasati was one of the simplest and most effective means for realizing emptiness. We could move from the vantage point of the thirteenth back through the twelve previous contemplations and see impermanence and emptiness in all of them.

I remember in particular the moment when we focused on the first contemplation, on the breath itself. I was sitting and listening meditatively as he instructed me. "There is no question," he said, "that breathing is taking place. Can you see that there is no breather to be found anywhere? The body is empty, the breath is empty, and you are empty."

He meant that all these phenomena are empty of self or anything belonging to the self; they are impermanent. They arise by given conditions, and when those conditions change, they pass away. The concept of impermanence in this contemplation actually encompasses the other laws of wisdom, that all phenomena are unsatisfactory and lack an abiding self. The simple vehicle of the breath takes the practitioner from calming the mind all the way to the deepest wisdom, to nirvana.

To say so much, of course, is to get way ahead of my story, but it is necessary to give some idea of what happened to me on that day. It wasn't just what Ajahn Buddhadasa said but also the way he said it, his insistence and his conviction. He let me see that because the breath is so unassuming, I had been undervaluing it. I was looking for a complicated path to enlightenment, when this simple one was right before me.

He argued that the breath was an ideal vehicle for teaching Buddhism in the West; it didn't carry the cultural baggage that mantras, koans, and other methods do. He also argued that this sutra was directly related to the *Satipatthana Sutra*, considered in the Theravada tradition to be the core of the Buddha's meditation teaching. The *Anapanasati Sutra* covers the same material in a more streamlined way, he said, and examines it with the help of conscious breathing. I left Thailand on that occasion with a new and clearer focus to my practice.

That was one of those moments in my life when many things came together. For years I had been a natural foods enthusiast and had practiced and was still practicing yoga, an ancient discipline that gives great attention to the breathing. I began to see that one thing that had always attracted me about the teachings of Thich Nhat Hanh was his recognition of the special nature of breathing. Time that I later spent with him on three long retreats was equally important in helping me grasp the full implications of the Buddha's teaching on breath awareness.

Thich Nhat Hanh's lineage draws on both Theravada and Mahayana teachings, and he is quietly and gently on fire with enthusiasm for this practice. He more than anyone else demonstrates the importance of bringing breath awareness into daily life, of staying awake in the midst of all our activities. He is unrelenting in his teaching, and it took such a strong message to get through to me.

This intense focus on the breathing connected with Soto Zen, with the work I had done with Katagiri Roshi and through him Suzuki Roshi, author of the seminal text *Zen Mind, Beginner's Mind*. Soto Zen emphasizes full attention to breathing and posture; all the wisdom one needs will be a natural outcome of such complete presence. The *Anapanasati Sutra*—though it can be used as a systematic course of contemplations—is also a blueprint of the way in which that wisdom can arise.

I have always been interested in Dharma study—I believe that, put in proper perspective, study and practice become one—and have always loved the classic texts of Buddhism. It gives me great satisfaction to teach from a sutra that is more than twenty-five hundred years old, as vital and alive and important as when it was originally spoken. For nearly ten years, it has been the basis of my personal practice and my teaching, and it has proven inexhaustible as a means to examine the message of the Buddha.

But I need to say a few things about the text before we begin. Seen in one way, it is a program to follow, one that takes the meditator from the observation of a simple process in the body—the in-and-out breathing—all the way to full awakening and realization. That is the way some teachers use it, most notably, in my experience, Ajahn Buddhadasa.

But it is also true that much of what the sutra describes will turn up naturally if you just sit and follow the breathing, if you persist in that practice over the course of days and months and years. It is natural for your attention to deepen until it includes the whole body, and for that process gradually to calm the body. Once your attention is in the body, you begin to notice feelings and your mental reactions to them, which lead you into the mind as a vast realm to explore. Finally, if you're paying attention, you can't help noticing that all the phenomena you're observing arise and pass away, that they are impermanent and lack an essential core.

The sixteen contemplations, then, represent a natural process. They might not unfold in exactly that order, and some of them might stand out more than others. But most of these aspects of body and mind eventually, and quite naturally, show up if you sit and look into yourself over a period of time.

That isn't the same thing as training in each contemplation, where you persistently come back to the object of the contemplation and confine your attention to it no matter what else is going on. So you can use the sutra as a training program or as the description of a process, but, however you use it, you can't force these steps. They will happen in their own time; you can't bring them about. You can prepare the ground, certainly, and make a sincere effort, but ultimately your body and mind do what they want, and you won't have much say about it.

However you decide to use the sutra, it is best to know the whole thing from the start, to read the entire commentary as you begin—or continue—your practice. I introduce sitting and walking meditation early on so that you will have those practices to follow as you read. It isn't necessary to read the whole book before you begin to practice. You also don't need to have mastered one contemplation before you read about the next.

I would suggest that very early on—right after you've read the meditation instructions, perhaps—you read chapter 6, on bringing the practice into daily life. You might profitably read that chapter several times in the course of reading the book. When I teach at our center in Cambridge, I emphasize daily life right from the start. It is very important to understand that you're being introduced not to an esoteric practice that is divorced from the rest of your life but to a new way of living, in which attention to every moment is paramount. In that way, it is fine to skip ahead in the book. It is fine to read chapter 6 anytime.

The first four chapters deal with the sixteen contemplations of the sutra itself, which divide themselves, as I've said, into four sets of four. Chapter 5 describes a condensed method of practice, reducing the sixteen steps to two; you may well decide to practice that way, but even if you do, it will be a great help to read about all sixteen first. Chapter 6, as I said, discusses bringing the practice into daily life, and chapter 7 is a brief introduction to the subject of silence, which is where the whole practice is headed but also where it all begins. That, too, is a chapter that you can read anytime in the course of the book, though there is a certain logic to having it at the end.

Through the centuries, Buddhism has traveled to different countries and taken on the hues of various cultures. In America, where it has arrived primarily in recent years, it will influence— and be influenced by—our culture. But we have a unique opportunity, because all of the Buddhist traditions are present here, and we can learn from all of them. People attach to different forms and draw sectarian lines, but in the end the various traditions aren't essentially different.

I teach vipassana meditation in the Theravada tradition, but I believe the *Anapanasati Sutra* is valuable even for those who practice in other traditions. This sutra is a teaching of the Buddha, after all, and was meant for all his disciples. vipassana meditators can use it as a training manual or as a reference text. Zen practitioners—who are given much less detailed guidance in their meditation instructions—can read it as an outline of what may happen in their practice. Those who meditate in the Tibetan tradition can use it in that way too. The *Anapanasati Sutra* is helpful for anyone who is attracted to the breath as an object of awareness.

Like many ancient texts, the sutra includes repetition and obscure and difficult passages. It is actually a whole study in itself. Since this book is intended as a manual for practice, not a scholarly commentary, I include at this point only the small section that highlights the teachings I will offer. The full text is in the appendix, and I will refer to parts of it in the teaching that follows.

In any case, let us read the words of the Buddha.

A N A P A N A S A T I   S U T R A

The meditator, having gone to the forest, to the shade of a tree, or to an empty building, sits down with legs folded crosswise, body held erect, and sets mindfulness to the fore. Always mindful, the meditator breathes in; mindful, the meditator breathes out.

The sixteen contemplations:

F I R S T   T E T R A D   (B O D Y   G R O U P)

1. While breathing in long, one knows: "I breathe in long." While breathing out long, one knows: "I breathe out long."

2. While breathing in short, one knows: "I breathe in short." While breathing out short, one knows: "I breathe out short."

3. One trains oneself: "Sensitive to the whole body, I breathe in. Sensitive to the whole body, I breathe out."

4. One trains oneself: "Calming the whole body, I breathe in. Calming the whole body, I breathe out."

SECOND TETRAD (FEELINGS GROUP)

5. One trains oneself: "Sensitive to rapture, I breathe in. Sensitive to rapture, I breathe out."

6. One trains oneself: "Sensitive to pleasure, I breathe in. Sensitive to pleasure, I breathe out."

7. One trains oneself: "Sensitive to mental processes, I breathe in. Sensitive to mental processes, I breathe out."

8. One trains oneself: "Calming mental processes, I breathe in. Calming mental processes, I breathe out."

THIRD TETRAD (MIND GROUP)

9. One trains oneself: "Sensitive to the mind, I breathe in. Sensitive to the mind, I breathe out."

10. One trains oneself: "Gladdening the mind, I breathe in. Gladdening the mind, I breathe out."

11. One trains oneself: "Steadying the mind, I breathe in. Steadying the mind, I breathe out."

12. One trains oneself: "Liberating the mind, I breathe in. Liberating the mind, I breathe out."

FOURTH TETRAD (WISDOM GROUP)

13. One trains oneself: "Focusing on impermanence, I breathe in. Focusing on impermanence, I breathe out."

14. One trains oneself: "Focusing on fading away, I breathe in. Focusing on fading away, I breathe out."

15. One trains oneself: "Focusing on cessation, I breathe in. Focusing on cessation, I breathe out."

16. One trains oneself: "Focusing on relinquishment, I breathe in. Focusing on relinquishment, I breathe out."

1

Breathing with the Body

WITNESS TO THE TEACHINGS

The *Anapanasati Sutra* begins with the words—familiar to anyone who has studied the original teachings of the Buddha—"I have heard" (often translated "Thus have I heard"). Ananda is speaking, the Buddha's cousin and one of his closest disciples. He is using this phrase to depersonalize the teachings—it is not I who is speaking—but also to legitimize and give them authority: this is from the Buddha.

For the first twenty years of his teaching, the Buddha used various attendants, but he decided finally to settle on just one. His followers were human beings, not saints, so there was a certain amount of competition and jockeying for position. Ananda didn't enter into that, so the Buddha chose him.

Ananda set some interesting conditions. He knew that the Buddha would be well received wherever he went—going into the best homes, being offered the best food and robes—and worried that such temptations would endanger his practice, so he asked to be left out of all that. He also made it a condition that if he ever felt any confusion about a Dharma talk, the Buddha would continue to answer his questions until he was sure he knew what was meant. If he ever missed a talk, the Buddha would repeat it for him.

Like many of the ancients—this was the period of the oral tradition—Ananda had a colossal memory. Three months after the Buddha died, there was a meeting of enlightened meditators to put together the essence of his teachings, and Ananda was central because he had heard and understood everything. All of the meditators had to agree to a sutra before it was admitted to the teachings. The words *Thus have I heard* became a seal of approval.

Bhikkhus is the word that the Buddha used to address his listeners, and though that word is normally translated "monks," the teachings were actually meant for laypeople as well. This term addresses itself to all serious practitioners. At the practice periods where his talks were given, senior monks instructed newer ones in groups of ten, twenty, thirty, or forty. A community, or sangha, had formed: a group of humans trying to deal, as we all do, with the fact that our minds produce suffering. An ideal sangha—as this one certainly was—includes members with some degree of awakening.

It is common even nowadays for Dharma centers to schedule three-month retreats. That tradition harkens back to the rainy season in India, which lasted roughly three months. Because of the steady rains, the farmers were working hard and travelers couldn't go anywhere. It was a good time for intensive practice. At the end of three months there was a Pavarana ceremony, which was a chance for monks to get instruction and to assess how they had done.

The Buddha at this particular ceremony said that things were going so well—the practitioners were practicing so diligently— that he would stay an extra month. Word got out, and monks from all over the country came to practice with him. At the end of that month, on the full moon day, he gave another talk; he began by speaking of various degrees of attainment and of the different practices that monks were engaged in. At the end of that list, he mentioned the subject of the sutra and the basis for our whole practice: "In this community of monks there are monks who remain devoted to the mindfulness of in-and-out breathing."

Any of the practices that the Buddha mentioned could have been the subject of endless explication. He was an extremely skillful teacher and used different methods depending on the group he was addressing. Basically, though, there is just one teaching—the Four Noble Truths—and all of the Buddha's other teachings fit within that framework: there is suffering; there is a cause for that suffering; there is an end to it, and there is a means to that end. He had often spoken before of working with the breathing, but on this occasion he put together all of the essential aspects of his teaching on this subject. He obviously believed this teaching to have great potential, giving rise, ultimately, to "clear knowing and release."

At the end of his introduction, the Buddha gives the simple instructions that form the basis for breath meditation. There is much more to say, of course, but also nothing more; if we could observe these instructions, the rest of the practice would follow.

"The meditator, having gone to the forest, to the shade of a tree, or to an empty building, sits down with legs folded crosswise, body held erect, and sets mindfulness to the fore. Always mindful, the meditator breathes in; mindful, the meditator breathes out."

When he mentions the forest, or the shade of a tree, the Buddha means that we should remove ourselves from familiar settings, which we have generally set up as places of craving and attachment (in our case, a refrigerator full of food, a television, stereo, shelves of books . . .). Most of us, of course, choose the empty building; that might be a place like a meditation center or a monastery, where people come for periods of intensive practice. It might also be a particular place in your house or apartment that you've set aside, one that is empty of your usual distractions.

Having a place free of distractions is especially helpful for new meditators, like training wheels on a child's bike or water wings for a new swimmer. Though correct practice is to be mindful everywhere—to take our practice into every aspect of daily

life—it is always helpful to have a safe and protected place desig-
nated for meditation.

The Buddha mentions a cross-legged posture. That has been a
traditional way to sit in the East, and for the purposes of meditation—with the weight resting like a stool on three points (two
knees and the buttocks)—it is ideal. Some people in the West
accomplish the same thing with a kneeling posture—using a
cushion or a bench—or sitting in a chair. The key factors are
comfort and stability. This is the beginning of a process known
as acquiring a seat, about which we will have more to say. The
first step in that process is to find a stable sitting posture that is
right for you.

Some students wonder if "cross-legged posture" refers to the
full-lotus position (each foot resting on the opposite thigh) or the
half lotus (one foot resting on the opposite thigh). Probably the
Buddha did mean the full lotus, and there is no question that it is
an extremely stable posture, perhaps the ideal one. I myself had
a teacher who thought the full lotus extremely important, and
who asked me to master it. It took me ten years. The first year I
couldn't even get into it. The next I could hold it for perhaps five
minutes. He also felt that I was too bookish, so he allowed me to
study every day for as long as I could hold the full lotus. That
was a great way to cut down on my reading.

Now the full lotus is quite comfortable for me, the most comfortable posture for sitting. But my own judgment is that it usually isn't worth a new student's trying so hard to learn it
(although, if you can assume the full lotus when you begin, it is
a good idea to sit that way and let the posture mature). If it sets
up an unrealistic goal, it can become an occasion for suffering
and a distraction from the real purpose of dharma practice. It can
too easily be in the service of the ego. Years after I had mastered
the full lotus, another teacher walked by while I was sitting,
tapped on my shoulder, and gestured toward my full lotus. "That
is the whole problem for you." And it can be a problem if it
becomes something you attach to.

The simple act of sitting in a stable upright posture with calmness and dignity has an importance all its own. The complete absence of movement is as much an expressive act as dance or martial arts. If we can sit like a Buddha, perhaps we can discover our Buddha nature. Such dignity has nothing to do with self-image and is in no way an affectation.

Picture a tree in a powerful storm, with high winds and heavy rain. The tree is blown back and forth by the wind, often looking as if it will blow over, but it doesn't, because it has deep roots. In our practice, the deep roots are a stable sitting posture—that's what acquiring a seat is all about, developing composure and stability—and the storm can be a powerful emotion, like fear or loneliness or anger.

We think of emotions as being in the mind, but the body and mind, though distinguishable, are interrelated, and the mind is also a crucial factor in developing a stable sitting posture. Once you have done that, you can be with whatever storm comes up; you can really experience your emotions, which is the key to becoming free from them.

The sitting posture is not an incidental factor but a vital part of the practice. Having a firm physical foundation to support the work of mindfulness can be crucial in helping our practice to mature. Of course, finally, and in a profound way—as we will see as we penetrate more deeply into the sutra—it is the mind that must sit in the full lotus.

Students often ask whether the eyes should be open or closed. In the Theravada—vipassana—tradition, we tend to sit with the eyes closed. Those in other traditions—Zen or Tibetan Buddhism—sit with the eyes open, or half-open. The advocates of the eyes-closed school say that if your eyes are open, there are too many distractions. The eyes-open school says that if your eyes are closed, fantasies arise, or you get sleepy. I have never found either of these things to be true. Most important is not to make a problem of it or allow it to become a distraction. Find a way that is right for you, and practice that.

Try to be straight and comfortable, relaxed and balanced. This isn't a mindless rigidity, which locks itself at the base of the spine and doesn't give the posture another thought, but a relaxed aware straightness, an uprightness that emerges from within. An erect posture makes the breathing easier, and ease of breathing relaxes the body. These two factors feed on each other.

Once you have established a stable posture, the Buddha says, you should arouse mindfulness.

PRACTICE AS INTIMACY

Mindfulness is a term that is used a great deal in the *Anapanasati Sutra*, and it would be helpful to understand it before we go on. We human beings have an extraordinary capacity, which we sometimes take for granted until it is called to our attention: unlike other beings in the world who are living out their lives, we have the ability to be conscious of that process as we do so.

Mindfulness is often likened to a mirror; it simply reflects what is there. It is not a process of thinking; it is preconceptual, before thought. One can be mindful of thought. There is all the difference in the world between thinking and knowing that thought is happening, as thoughts chase each other through the mind and the process is mirrored back to us.

The only time that mindfulness can happen is in the present moment; if you are thinking of the past, that is memory. It is possible to be mindful of memory, of course, but such mindfulness can only happen in the present.

Mindfulness is unbiased. It is not for or against anything, just like a mirror, which does not judge what it reflects. Mindfulness has no goal other than the seeing itself. It doesn't try to add to what's happening or subtract from it, to improve it in any way.

It isn't detached, like a person standing on a hill far away from an experience, observing it with binoculars. It is a form of participation—you are fully living out your life, but you are awake in the midst of it—and it is not limited to the meditation hall. It can be used on a simple process like the breathing, or on highly charged and unpleasant emotions like fear or loneliness. It can also follow us into the ordinary life situations that make up our day. Eventually, it becomes more a way of living than a technique.

One word that I personally have come to associate with mindful living is *intimacy*. The great thirteenth-century Japanese Zen teacher Dogen was once asked, "What is the awakened mind?" and he answered, "The mind that is intimate with all things." To take a simple example: You're walking in the woods and your attention is drawn to a beautiful tree or a flower. The usual human reaction is to set the mind working, "What a beautiful tree, I wonder how long it's been here, I wonder how often people notice it, I really should write a poem. . . ."

The way of mindfulness would be just to see the tree. As we will discuss later, you might focus on the breath for a few moments, so that the thinking calms itself. Then as you gaze at the tree there is nothing between you and it. There is no separation. You are at one with it.

This is not, as people sometimes believe, to demean thinking. Thinking is a marvelous human activity; the Buddha's teachings themselves—among many other human marvels—would be impossible without it. But thinking often comes between us and our experience. Inasmuch as it does, we are not intimate with that moment. We are not mindful.

Mindfulness does not just belong to inspiring moments in nature. We often—as we emphasize on retreats—practice with the most mundane tasks, taking out the garbage, cleaning the toilet. An example from my own life is that I have gradually become aware, in recent years, that I whistle as I wash the dishes. Not only that, but the songs I whistle tend to be old ones, from the 1950s.

What I gradually realized was that when I was a teenager, I shared the dishwashing with my sister, and whatever I might think now of simple housekeeping tasks, in those days I found them a pain. To get myself through the dishes, I would whistle. And here I am, still whistling the same tunes all these years later.

The task of mindfulness is not to strong-arm yourself into some rigid attitude: "I have failed in my practice; I will not whistle again for the remainder of my adult life." It is just to see that whistling, or singing, or thinking, is separating you from your experience. Once I saw that, I could whistle again. The whistling was no longer a shield obstructing my raw contact with dishwashing. These were no longer two activities colliding with each other. The two things had become one.

There is a centuries-old koan that I often use in my teaching. Koans come out of the Zen tradition and are questions that students meditate on to further their practice. In the old Zen monasteries, the temperature could be a major factor; people practiced year-round, and of course there was no central heating or air conditioning. So the question arose, "How do you practice when you're extremely hot or extremely cold?"

Any number of answers were given through the years. "Go to the place where there is no hot or cold." Where might that be? the student wonders. And the teacher answers, enigmatically, "Hot Buddha. Cold Buddha." A further amplification might be, "Hot kills. Cold kills. Don't make hot, don't make cold."

The teaching here concerns the same tendency we have already mentioned, to add concepts to our experience and make it other than it is. The fact is that there is a certain temperature—you're sitting with sweat pouring down your face, or with your teeth chattering—and that is the moment for you, those particular sensations. As soon as you add concepts to the discomfort, torment begins: What if I get dehydrated? What if I get heat prostration? Or what if I get frostbite? Die of exposure? Why is it so cold when it's only September? Why didn't I stay home so I wouldn't have this problem at all?

There are obviously certain extreme conditions that require some action, and a mindful person would be the first to notice them. But most of the time we are within a normal range of temperatures, and the task of mindfulness is to be intimate with the experience, really to feel the sweat pouring down the face or the body shivering. When the Buddha is hot, he sweats; when cold, he shivers.

Sometimes we have the mistaken idea that a truly enlightened being wouldn't be subject to such conditions. The Buddha wouldn't notice heat or cold. Actually, almost the opposite is true. He would be aware of them to an extraordinary degree. He would feel all of their subtle gradations. But he wouldn't make anything more out of them. They would be just what they are.

The subject of intimacy often comes up in terms of relationship, of course, and has become a contemporary obsession. People are sometimes desperate to experience intimacy. But it is extremely difficult to be intimate with someone else until you've been intimate with yourself, and the same kind of thought processes interfere with relationships that interfere with everything else in our life. We build up images of ourselves and of the other, and in a typical interaction, the real people don't meet at all. Practice breaks through all that, breaks through these images to what is really happening in the moment. Real intimacy does not look for some particular experience but sees things as they are.

Finally, enlightenment is the experience of intimacy with the entire universe. There is no separation whatsoever. You totally disappear in the process of uniting with the raw content of the present moment. And because you do, you have never been more alive. A famous Tibetan master, Kalu Rinpoche, expressed this truth beautifully:

> We live in illusion
> And the appearance of things.
> There is a reality.
> We are that reality.
>
> When you understand this
> You see that you are nothing.
> And being nothing,
> You are everything.
> That is all.

THE SOURCE OF LIFE

This quality of mindfulness, of just being with an experience, is what the meditator arouses when assuming the seated posture. At first the meditator brings his or her awareness to an extremely simple process.

"Always mindful, the meditator breathes in; mindful, the meditator breathes out."

It sounds simple, of course, but it's actually—as anyone knows who has tried it—a profound and difficult practice. The fact is that when we focus on the breath, we are focusing on the life force. Life begins with our first breath and will end after our last. To contemplate breathing is to contemplate life itself.

An ancient teaching from India points to this truth. There was a conference of all the human faculties, all the senses, which in the Indian tradition are six: the five senses plus the mind. As at many meetings, they first had to decide who would be in charge. Sight popped up and put in its bid, creating beautiful images that had everyone enraptured. Smell arose and created powerful and haunting aromas that left everyone tingling with anticipation. But taste could top that, with astounding and delectable flavors from all the world's cuisines. Hearing created exquisite harmonies that brought everyone to tears, and the body brought on physical sensations that had everyone in ecstasy, and the mind spun out intellectual theories that took on beauty by the depths of the truths they expressed.

Along came the breath—not even one of the senses!—and said it wanted to be in charge. All it could present was the simple in-and-out breath, not terribly impressive in the face of everything else. No one even noticed it. The other senses got into a tremendous argument about which one of them would be chosen. The breath in its disappointment began walking away. And the images began to fade, the tastes lost their savor, the sounds diminished. . . . "Wait," the senses called out. "Come back. You can lead. We need you." And the breath came back and took its proper place.

Sometimes, especially when people are new to the practice, they say they're bored with watching the breathing. I try to use this story to awaken their interest, but occasionally I have to resort to more extreme measures. One new meditator kept coming to interviews with a chronic lament, "The breath is so *bor*ing." Finally I asked him if he'd ever heard of Brooklyn yoga. He said no. I told him to close his mouth tight and close off both nostrils with his fingers. We sat that way for some time until, finally, he let go of his nose and gasped for air. "Was that breath boring?" I said.

Ancient India had a tremendous respect for the breath, a deep understanding of its powerful effect on the body and mind. Sciences of the breath developed. In fact, all of the Indian spiritual sciences had some form of *pranayama*, which is usually translated "breath control," though those words don't capture its essence. In our sutra, the Pali word *anapanasati* is composed in part of *ana*, which is the life energy as it comes in, and *apana*, the waste as it is expelled. Put together, they form *anapana*. The sutra concerns the awareness of that entire process.

Most forms of pranayama, yogic breathing, involve controlling the breath. *Anapanasati* accomplishes some of the same things—it is a kind of Buddhist science of breath—by letting the breath be as it is, by surrendering to the process. There is no question that if this practice is followed over a period of time— months and years—the quality of the breathing does improve; it becomes fuller, deeper, and calmer, with consequences both physical and psychological.

We're all breathing. The instruction is just to know that we are, not in an intellectual sense, but to be aware of the simple sensation, the in-breath and the out-breath. Even in this first instruction, we are learning something extremely important, to allow the breathing to follow its own nature, to breathe itself. We are not trying to make the breath deep or keep it shallow. We are seeing how it is.

That flies in the face of our lifelong conditioning to control, direct, and orchestrate everything. We're terrified of chaos, afraid that if we don't keep things in their place they will fall apart. Most of us are quite good at controlling, and what we'd really like is to be even better at it. Our tendency is to ride the breath, push it along, help it out, especially when we hear that the breath is part of this marvelous sutra, that it is the life force itself and can lead us to enlightenment. All that is like a clarion call to the ego, which begins to tell the breath how to be. We hear that a deep breath relaxes the body and figure that an accomplished meditator will be breathing deeply all the time, so—sometimes very subtly—we try to make the breath a little deeper.

That isn't the instruction. The instruction is to let it be, to surrender to the breathing. We are learning even in this first instruction the art of surrender, which is central to our Dharma practice.

If we can learn to allow the breath to unfold naturally, without tampering with it, then in time we may be able to do that with other aspects of our experience: we might learn to let the feelings be, let the mind be. We do a great deal more controlling of the mind, because we're afraid of what might turn up. But it is through letting the mind be that we eventually learn how to relax and let go into freedom, what Buddhism sometimes calls our true nature, what Zen refers to as "your face before your parents were born." A famous Zen koan asks the practitioner to show his teacher that face. *Anapanasati* gets at the same thing with the help of conscious breathing.

If you've sat with the breath for even a few minutes, you've seen that this practice is an open invitation for everything inside you to come up. You see your wild mind, which we all have, and which can be quite overwhelming at first. It has been there all along, of course, but this concentration has brought it into relief.

The ultimate goal—though this is no easy thing and takes time to develop—is to allow everything to come up, with all its energy: all of, for instance, your anger and loneliness and despair, to allow these things to arise and be transformed by the light of awareness. There is tremendous energy in these states, and much of the time we suppress them, so that we not only lose all the energy that is in them but also expend a great deal keeping them down. What we gradually learn is to let these things come up and be transformed, to release their energy. You don't solve your problems in this practice, it is sometimes said, you dissolve them.

But the wild mind that we all confront when we start discourages many practitioners. Buddhist tradition calls it monkey mind, like a drunken monkey swinging through the jungle endlessly looking for bigger and better bananas. Sometimes it seems like a frantic cage full of monkeys. But for some years, ever since a simple experience I had, I have used a different metaphor.

DOGGY MIND

One time when I was visiting a friend, he kept playing with his dog, throwing a plastic bone for the dog to go fetch. It not only wasn't a real bone, it wasn't even a convincing fake; pieces of meat were painted on the plastic. Yet no matter how many times he threw the bone, the dog ran after it, with great excitement. He kept chasing this plastic bone, which had no nourishment whatsoever, as if it could somehow satisfy him. Suddenly I realized: that's my mind, chasing after thoughts. The mind doesn't think it's chasing a plastic bone with pieces of meat painted on it, of course. It thinks it's pursuing something that will have a vital effect on its life. But if we look more closely at the objects that the mind chases, we notice a similar lack of nourishment.

In contrast to that, think of a lion. Can you imagine how a lion—sitting in that majestic way they have—would react if you threw him a bone (especially a plastic one)? He wouldn't even notice. He'd just stare at you. Lions stay focused on the source. That's the attitude we need to have, sitting with that deep calm, that steadiness of purpose, not chasing after every bone that flies our way. We need to develop lion mind.

Some years ago I had an experience that, when I thought about it later, left me quite sheepish and let me know just how strong these habitual tendencies of the mind are. I was at the Insight Meditation Society on a self-retreat, meditating in my room at about 11:30 in the morning. It was roughly the middle of the retreat, and in that particular sitting my mind got extremely still, full of joy and bliss and peace. I began to have the feeling: *This is it. This is what I've been reading about for years, hoping with all my heart to achieve. Full and total enlightenment. It's right around the corner....*

At which point the lunch bell rang—they have a kind of gong that they ring there, which gives off a beautiful sound as the ringer walks through the halls—and without hesitating I unfolded my legs, stood up, and walked downstairs to get my rice and vegetables. It was only afterward that I said to myself, Hey, wait a minute. No matter how you look at that story, one fact is clear. I preferred a good meal to enlightenment.

That reminded me of a story I'd once heard about a ritual theater they have in Japan. They dress monkeys in costumes and teach them to act out roles in classical dramas, what would probably correspond to Shakespeare for us. It's all a huge put-on. And in one noted play, one of the most famous scenes in all of Japanese drama, two monkeys were on the stage, one playing a general, one an emperor, in an extremely dramatic confrontation. Then somebody from the audience threw a banana on the stage. So much for great moments in drama.

That's the way our minds work. We can be in the loftiest moods, contemplating the ultimate truths of the cosmos, but just ring the dinner bell—throw us a banana—and it all goes up in smoke. "If the least like or dislike arises," as Dogen says, "the mind is lost in confusion."

So our practice is to try to go from doggy mind to something more like lion mind, in which there is a deep steadiness. In the Thai tradition, they use the metaphor of different kinds of houses, starting with twig huts, then bamboo, moving on to stones or brick. When conditions are difficult—a storm is raging—you have that solid house to go to for protection. When you're just starting, before you've developed any calm, it's as if you're homeless. You have no shelter at all.

A number of beginning students ask where in the body they should follow the breath. I've read widely in the Buddha's teachings and consulted a number of scholars, and nowhere does he give a precise answer to this question. Nevertheless, a number of traditional teachers are very specific. Some say the place to follow it is the abdomen, others say the nostrils or chest region. As far as I'm concerned, they are all right. It is really just a matter of individual preference.

Having worked with any number of students through the years, I feel that meditators should follow the breathing where it seems most vivid and comfortable to them, where it is most likely to hold their attention. None of these places will always, in every sitting, remain the most vivid. But it is important not to keep jumping from one to another, feeding an already restless mind. Station your attention at the nose, chest, or abdomen, and remain there with some consistency. As the practice matures, it may no longer be necessary to pinpoint your attention. You can be with the breath as it emerges and disappears throughout the body.

A number of adjunct techniques have developed through the centuries. The mind keeps flying off to one thing after another, and sometimes it helps to give it something to do. One simple technique is silent counting. Numbering either the in-breath or the out-breath, start with one and count up to ten. For some people, one or the other of these is more vivid and easier to follow. If that is true for you, begin with whichever is consistently more accessible. When you reach ten breaths, start back at one. If your mind wanders and you lose count, start back at one. Don't torture yourself, so that you're constantly failing and getting down on yourself. Make it more playful than that, like a kid's game.

Once you can do, say, ten sets of ten—though this is not a hard-and-fast rule—you might switch to the other breath, the one that was less vivid. Ten sets of ten of those and you might give up counting, just work with the breath. If ten breaths are too hard for you to reach, start with five and work up to ten. There are no rules about any of this. It's just a matter of what helps you.

Obviously, counting was chosen because it's so simple a mental procedure. There is no significance in what number you're saying, or how high you've gotten; the idea is for the mind, the number, and the breath to become one. Another possibility is to use what is called a *parikamma*, a word used as a meditation theme. In Thailand there is much use of *Buddho*, an epithet for the Buddha—"the one who knows"—splitting it on the in-and-out breath. Bud-dho. Some Westerners don't feel comfortable with this word because it's foreign. The words *in* and *out* can be just as effective.

Thich Nhat Hanh has introduced many beautiful *gathas*, or dharmic poems, which when keyed to the breath are another way to stabilize our attention. In my own teaching, I favor weaning the meditator away from any conceptual aids as soon as possible, turning to bare unmediated attention to the breath. But each person's practice needs to unfold in its own unique manner.

For some people, breathing isn't a terribly pleasant process. A lifetime of faulty breathing, often accompanied by emotional blockages, has made the breath an unattractive object of attention, resulting in a great deal of fantasy or other forms of distraction. Ajahn Buddhadasa suggests washing the nostrils before you meditate in the morning, with perhaps a quarter of a teaspoon of salt in a glass of tepid water, snuffing it in through each nostril, to make the nasal linings more sensitive. It might also help to practice hatha yoga, t'ai chi, or other physical disciplines that focus on the breathing. Anything that helps you breathe more easily will make the breath a more attractive object of attention.

Finally, you need to develop a certain devotion to your meditation object. We all start off somewhat skeptically, but if this practice is right for you, there comes a time when you simply give yourself over to it. The breath is an object that the Buddha often meditated on. It is what he used to help him achieve enlightenment. He continued to practice with it for years after his awakening. The breath, as we gradually discover, is a whole world. It is easily worth a lifetime of study.

And it is a superb aid in helping us stay in the present moment. The Thai teacher Ajahn Chah used to repeat the same advice to us, almost like a mantra, no matter what came up: Keep it simple, and stick to the present moment. Those words are equally valuable to a beginner just starting out and to the most advanced practitioner reading this book. They are still valuable for me. If you are learning about meditation for the first time, you may decide that you might want to try to sit now, for ten minutes or so. Fine. But don't think of it as ten minutes. Just sit for this moment. Then the next moment. And so on.

I had an extremely dramatic teaching of the importance of staying in the present moment during the year that I spent in Korea. I had been there roughly two months, during which my teacher had taken me and a couple of American monks on a walking tour of the country's monasteries. I had also—as a layperson and a former university professor—done some lecturing in Seoul on Zen in America, Zen practice for laypeople. My teacher was trying to encourage lay practice and had bought me a tailored three-piece suit so that I would impress the Koreans.

After those two months, he got special permission for me to do a ninety-day retreat at the Su Duk Sah monastery. Sixty monks were taking part, including the two Americans I'd been traveling with. I was the only layperson. But my teacher had assured those running the retreat that I would be able to handle it and that I would follow the rules. There was a certain scepticism among the Korean monks, especially when I arrived in that three-piece suit. "You practice gentleman style," they said, joking with me. "Now you'll have to practice our style."

In fact, the schedule was extremely difficult, and within ten days all but fourteen of the monks had dropped out. We woke up every day at 3:00 A.M., and would sit around the clock—fifty minutes of sitting followed by ten minutes of brisk walking—until 11:00 P.M. We actually slept in the same places we sat, our sitting mats opening out into sleeping mats. We also ate there, two meals of rice and vegetables every day, some miso broth at night. I had done seven-day *sesshins* before, but this was the longest and most difficult retreat I had ever been on.

As we approached the forty-five-day mark, we heard that it was an ancient tradition at that monastery to spend one week in the middle of the ninety days without any sleep at all. When the other Americans and I heard that, we got slightly hysterical, angry and frightened. No one had told us about that tradition. It sounded absurd to us, positively inhumane. We considered leaving. But we knew we couldn't, because our teacher had expressed such confidence in us. We decided we just had to do it.

The first day of the week without sleep was terrible. One monk walked around with what they called the stick of compassion, with which he whacked our shoulders to keep us awake. We weren't allowed to wander off at breaks, because the temptation to lie down for a nap would have been unbearable. By the time we entered into the early hours of the morning, during which I would normally have been getting my few hours of sleep, I was absolutely miserable.

On the second day I asked for an interview with the Zen master, a ninety-four-year-old man named Hae Am Su Nim, who was so frail that he had to be carried in and out on his mat. He was not actually on the retreat but had done it many times in the past. I told him what a difficult time I was having. He said that a week without sleep could definitely be done. It had been done by many others before me. The problem was that, in addition to my fatigue, I was carrying around an extra burden: the concept of seven days without sleep. I would be able to get through the week, he said, if I would put that burden down, if I took every activity moment by moment, breath by breath, giving full attention to whatever it was. Every sitting period, every walking period, every break, every meal. Just stay in the moment, and I would be fine.

He was right. The week was still difficult—I actually got to a point where I was hallucinating—but I was able to get through it.

My concentration increased dramatically, as did my confidence in sitting. As our presence in meditation deepens, we actually need less sleep.

I myself don't use such practices in my teaching; they are brutal on the body, and I prefer to let my students' capacities develop more gradually. But the advice that monk gave me that day has stayed with me ever since and helped me in countless situations. It will help you in whatever situations you face, on the cushion and elsewhere.

No one ever said it better than Ajahn Chah. Keep it simple, and stick to the present moment.

TAKING THE BREATH FOR A WALK

In all of the classes I teach, in addition to giving instructions for sitting, I always teach walking meditation. On the one hand—in a class or on retreat—it is a break from the sitting, a chance to stand and get the blood circulating again. But it is also a vital and important part of the practice, especially in the Theravada tradition, where monks often spend hours doing it.

The Buddha said that it is important to develop mindfulness in all four postures: sitting, standing, walking, and lying down. This practice brings mindfulness to walking, and though we often do a slow stylized form of it, you can take the mindfulness you develop into all of the walking you do in your life: around the house, outside, even the longer walking—or running—that you might do for exercise. In taking the practice into daily life, walking is extremely important because it is a form of meditation in motion, and also because we spend so much of our lives doing it.

I teach two methods of formal walking and will discuss the simpler one first. You begin by choosing a walking track, an unencumbered path where you can take fifteen to twenty steps (the steps themselves are quite small). Stand in a balanced posture and notice that you are breathing, just as you have been doing while sitting. You can clasp your hands in front of you if that feels comfortable. Some people clasp them behind the back; others just let their arms hang at their sides.

It is helpful if your body is upright—not leaning in any direction—and relaxed. If you feel tension in any part of the body, just bring mindfulness to it and that will usually take care of it. The eyes are open but not staring. Try to maintain a soft gaze.

To begin, wait for an in-breath. As it arises, raise the right foot, heel first, then the sole of the foot, then the toes. Move the foot forward as the breath continues, and as you exhale, place it on the ground, finishing the step. The heel of the stepping foot should be just ahead of the toes of the other one. Then wait for the next inhalation and take the same kind of step with the left foot.

The breath sets the pace, so if you are breathing slowly—as you are likely to be if you have been sitting—you will move quite slowly. The challenge is to let the breath lead and to synchronize the movements of the legs with it. This requires close attention and doesn't leave much room for distraction. It is excellent practice in *not* controlling the breath, a skill that is valuable for sitting practice as well.

At the end of the walking track, stand and breathe mindfully for a few moments, then turn and do the same kind of walking in the other direction. If, as you walk, some preoccupation takes over the mind, pulling your attention away from the walking again and again, you may wish to come to a halt and turn to the breath—along with the preoccupation itself—until the mind is clear.

Your primary attention is to the feet as they leave the ground, move, and touch the ground again. The breath is in the background, dictating the pace of these movements. You may want to focus on a larger area, like the whole leg. But your attention is to the act of walking.

The other method of walking meditation is slightly more complicated and, believe it or not, a little slower. When the in-breath arises, just raise the heel of the right foot, with the toes still lightly touching the ground. Leave your foot in this position as the exhalation takes place. Then, with the next in-breath, raise that foot, move it forward, and place it on the ground. With the exhalation, shift your weight to that foot, completing the step.

This method, since it is slightly more complex, requires more attention to subtle aspects of the breathing, and it allows more concentration to develop for some meditators.

The sensations you will notice during this slow walking are quite ordinary. People are often looking for Hollywoodish special effects in meditation and don't pick up on these subtle sensations at first; then, when they do, they wonder why they bothered. The question is: can we let them be the way they are, just the subtle sensations of slow walking, and take one step at a time?

Eventually, the sense of a leg and foot may disappear, and you will notice just the movement itself. It is extremely helpful to regard each step as an end in itself, not a segment of progress along the path. After all, in terms of transportation, our progress isn't terribly impressive. We're not really getting anywhere.

Another technique is to move at a normal pace and count the steps you take in the process of breathing, first on the inhalation (one, two, three), then the exhalation. Don't impose a pattern on the breath; just let it flow naturally. It is easy to get mechanical about this method, but the lungs' need for air may change during the course of a walk, so you will have to stay alert. At the beginning, the pace you walk will probably condition the breathing, but in time the breathing may begin to condition the walking. The two become integrated and make themselves into one process.

It is also possible to practice just with the breathing as you walk; whatever pace you're moving, make the breath the primary object of attention. You will notice the walking to some extent, of course, but keep coming back to the breathing. After you've been practicing breath awareness for some time, you may find that the breath and the sensations of the body become inseparable. There is a walking breathing body and the knowing of it.

I have always enjoyed natural walking as a form of meditation. The breath and body are a unified field, and I attend to this walking breathing body as I move around the house or go outside. This feeling isn't something to force; it will happen naturally over time, as you develop mindfulness. Walking will then become a much different activity in your life.

In our own cultural past, Thoreau was a great walker, and he spoke of the importance of mindfulness in walking.

> Of course, it is no use to direct our steps to the woods if they do not carry us thither. I am alarmed when it happens that I have walked a mile into the woods bodily, without getting there in spirit. In my afternoon walk I would fain forget all my morning occupations and my obligations to society, but it still happens sometimes that I can not easily shake the village. The thought of some work will run in my head and I am not where my body is—I am out of my senses. What business have I in the woods, if I am thinking of something out of the woods?"

Saint Francis of Assisi had a simpler way of putting it: "It is no use walking anywhere to preach unless our walking is our preaching."

The Buddha, too, spoke of the advantages of natural walking.

> These are the five rewards for one who practices walking meditation. . . . He can endure traveling by foot; he can endure exertion; he becomes free from disease; whatever he has eaten and drunk, chewed and savored, becomes well-digested; the concentration he wins while doing walking meditation lasts for a long time.

It is perhaps this concentration, and the joy of walking in such a state, that is the primary reward.

VARIETIES OF BREATHING

We have now arrived at the first contemplation of the sutra. In the Chinese tradition, the contemplations are numbered differently, with the simple awareness of breathing as number one, then with numbers two and three combined. I prefer the Theravadan order but generally teach the first two contemplations together.

1. While breathing in long, one knows: "I breathe in long." While breathing out long, one knows: "I breathe out long."

2. While breathing in short, one knows: "I breathe in short." While breathing out short, one knows: "I breathe out short."

These first two contemplations move from a simple awareness of breathing to the particular qualities of the breath, a change in focus that happens quite naturally. Most commentators agree that the Buddha meant more than long and short here; he was talking about all the qualities of the breath. As we become more familiar with breathing, we perceive subtle nuances in it.

Sometimes the breath is very fine, like silk or satin; it enters and exits freely. How wonderful just to be breathing! At other times it is coarse, more like burlap; it fights its way in and out. Sometimes the breath is so deep and smooth that it affects the whole body, relaxing us profoundly. Other times it's so short and pinched, hurried and agitated, that our minds and bodies are like that, restless and uncomfortable.

It's hard to know what comes first, whether the problem is in the breathing, the body, or the mind. Each part conditions the others. As we practice longer, we come to see that these distinctions are false anyway; these supposed parts of us are really just one thing. But the breath is an extremely sensitive psychic barometer.

One of the things you learn about this whole process—the conjunction of mind and body, with the breath as the meeting place—is that awareness has an extremely powerful effect on it. This isn't a matter of controlling, or attempting to change, the breath. But as you pay attention, the quality of the breathing changes, perhaps because thinking is diminished. The breath be-

comes deeper, finer, silkier, more enjoyable, and the body starts
to bear the fruits of that, to become more relaxed.

This isn't something to try for. Trying actually prevents it. It
just reflects the power of mindfulness. You find yourself growing
angry or worried; your heart starts to pound, your body to grow
tense; but if you can just be with the breath for a while—not
suppressing the emotion, but breathing with it—all that changes.
The mind grows calm. As the breath goes, so goes the body.
Something happens when mindfulness touches breathing. Its
quality changes for the better.

That is a part of what you learn from these first two contemplations, noting not just whether the breath is long or short but all
the other effects it has as well. This attention to the breath has
tremendous consequences.

But it is important to emphasize, in discussing the art of meditation (and the practice as you continue it becomes an art, with
many subtle nuances), that you shouldn't start out with some idea
of gaining. This is the deepest paradox in all of meditation: we
want to get somewhere—we wouldn't have taken up the practice
if we didn't—but the way to get there is just to be fully here. The
way to get from point A to point B is really to be at A. When we
follow the breathing in the hope of becoming something better,
we are compromising our connection to the present, which is all
we ever have. If your breathing is shallow, your mind and body
restless, let them be that way, for as long as they need to. Just
watch them.

The first law of Buddhism is that everything is constantly
changing. No one is saying that the breathing should be some
particular way all the time. If you find yourself disappointed with
your meditation, there's a good chance that some idea of gaining
is present. See that, and let it go. However your practice seems to
you, cherish it just the way it is. You may think that you want it
to change, but that act of acceptance is in itself a major change.

It has the dynamic power to take your mind into stability and serenity, which are at the core of the first four contemplations.

HITTING THE TARGET

One place where ideas of gaining typically come in, where people get obsessive about the practice, is in the task of staying with the breathing. We take a simple instruction and create a drama of success and failure around it: we're succeeding when we're with the breath, failing when we're not. Actually, the whole process is meditation: being with the breathing, drifting away, seeing that we've drifted away, gently coming back. It is extremely important to come back without blame, without judgment, without a feeling of failure. If you have to come back a thousand times in a five-minute period of sitting, just do it. It's not a problem unless you make it into one.

Each instance of seeing that you've been away is, after all, a moment of mindfulness, as well as a seed that increases the likelihood of such moments in the future. Best of all is to go beyond the whole mentality of success and failure, to understand that our lives are a series of alternations between various states. If you already had some kind of laser-like attention that never wavered, you wouldn't need to practice meditation at all. The object of these first two contemplations isn't to make your breathing perfect. It's to see how your breathing really is.

One summer morning some years ago I observed a master of Zen archery give a demonstration for the sangha. Nearly 150 people were present, in a large open field. He had set up a target and was in full Japanese regalia, with robes and wrist guards and all kinds of paraphernalia. There was an elaborate ceremony before the arrow would be released and—we all hoped—would hit the bullseye, all kinds of chanting and ritual gestures. The moment arrived, and we could feel the tension. The master pulled back the bowstring with the arrow. We were holding our breath. It seemed forever that he held it there. Then he suddenly shifted and shot it into the air. There was a huge groan from the crowd. The archer burst into laughter.

He was letting us know that the obsession with a target was not the point. We in the West have a very strong "in order to" mind. We want to go from A to B, B to C. Ideally we'd like to go from A straight to Z, get our Ph.D. the first day, skip all the steps in between. Enlightenment in one easy lesson. Our mind spends all its time calculating. Everything is a means to an end.

But that misses the point. Each breath moment is both a means and an end. We're not looking at the breath in order to get to enlightenment. We're just looking at the breath, rooted to it, sitting with it like a lion. Enlightenment, after all, is just one more bone. It's an idea we have.

The instruction is to disappear into the breathing and leave all the bones behind, all the preoccupations, worries, plans, fears, all the stuff that makes up the mind. And when we get caught up in them again, to return gently to the breath. Especially in the modern world, where everybody is so impressed with variety and complexity, so desperate to be entertained, it is a relief to settle into this simple repetitive act. The opportunity we have, of staying with the breathing, constantly coming back to it, is a chance to do one simple, ordinary thing well, to treat it with great care and respect.

Entering into this spirit of repetition can also be a wonderful lesson in simplicity, which is also desperately needed in the modern world. Many people come to meditation expecting some complex practice leading to an extraordinary experience. They can't believe they're just supposed to sit there and watch the breath. But when we learn to surrender to one simple object, we begin to see how useful this skill is in other aspects of our lives. How many times do we brush our teeth, go to the bathroom, put on our clothes, make the bed? Our days are dominated by such ordinary and repetitive activity, which we generally handle by going on automatic pilot. That means that we miss out on much of our lives. This practice teaches us to stay fresh in the midst of all routine activity, really to live our lives.

Practice with Ajahn Maha Boowa in Thailand provided dramatic training in this spirit. Each meditator was given a little hut, called a *kuti*, in the forest. The huts were all connected by pathways, and leaves fell from the trees all day long. Twice a day, morning and evening, we'd get a broom and sweep our path. Even as we were doing it, we'd see leaves starting to cover the place we'd already swept, giving us an opportunity to take joy in the job even as we watched it being undone. Much in our lives is like that, when you think about it.

I've given the instructions for meditation a staggering number of times. I usually manage to stay fresh in that situation, but I sometimes hear myself droning on in a metallic voice, and that is my reminder to wake up. I come back, the same way I come back to the breath. When I pay attention, the same old instructions take on a new life.

So the constant repetition of coming back to the breath has real value. Our wish always to hit the target, always be doing it right, is an obstacle. We start to blame ourselves: *I don't know how to do this, I'm a bad meditator, everybody else is concentrating but me. If only my mind didn't wander, I'd be able to practice.* But seeing that the mind has wandered *is* practice. If you continue for years, you'll have to come back, who knows, millions of times. So learning to come back gracefully is extremely important. Make it a dance, not a wrestling match.

Another aspect of the practice—and this is somewhat beyond the contemplation we're dealing with, though some of it is bound to happen even when you're just looking at the breath—is that we begin to see the nature of the bones we keep chasing. The core of the practice, once we've developed some concentration, will be to look at these bones. Certain things come up again and again. "He said, then she said, then I said, then we . . ." Or, "If that works out I might . . . , but on the other hand I could . . ." It's rather obvious, from the fact that these things keep coming up, that your obsessive thinking doesn't resolve them. They also don't usually involve the highest priorities of life. Maybe, when you see that, you won't chase after them quite so much. You'll see how futile it all is.

There's a word in the Yiddish language—*yenta*—that describes this phenomenon. A yenta is a neighborhood gossip, who knows everybody's business, always knows what's going on, is always trying to poke around and stir things up. You begin to notice that the mind is one big yenta, talking about others, berating itself, pointing out how it used to be better, seeing how it might improve. Life, on the other hand, keeps on being just the way it is. We begin to see that all our ideas about how it should be take up far too many of our precious breath moments. We need to begin just to see life—and accept it—as it is.

RESPECTING EACH MOMENT

In the tradition of Jewish mysticism, the Hassids believe that each person has been given a certain corner of the universe to take care of. You might be president of the United States or a clerk at the corner candy store, a mother of ten or a mechanic who lives alone in a small apartment, but everyone has a world, and whatever is in your life at a given moment is your world. For me, at this moment, it is trying to present these words clearly. For you it is trying to make sense of them. Our world is always present. This is our world, now.

It is therefore always appropriate to ask: What is my situation? What am I supposed to be doing, right here, right now? When you're in the car, your task is to drive. When your child comes to you with a problem, your task is to listen. Each moment has its own intelligence. Just as you follow the breathing, you direct yourself to that task. When you drift away you, come back. Again. And again.

As we begin to see clearly when we practice, the mind is chasing bones constantly, not just when we're sitting. Sometimes, if what you're doing is quite simple, you have a chance to examine that: What is it that keeps pulling me away? (It may be that there is something else that you need to do, or undo.) Other times, if what you're engaged in is vital and complicated, your task is to keep coming back to that. It's a matter of having respect for your activity. Ultimately, you're having respect for your life.

In some ways this entire practice, everything the Buddha said, is concerned with having respect—an infinite respect—for life. That's what living dharma is finally about. It's one of the things that Mother Teresa has shown us: that the poorest of the poor, in the last moments of their lives, are worthy of total regard. So are the most ordinary events in our lives.

Most of us respect some things and not others. We pay attention to an important business meeting but not to our children when they're talking to us. We watch the latest Hollywood blockbuster but don't listen to the birds in the trees. We exult in our good moods and try not to notice our bad ones. We're riveted to our tennis game but don't notice our footsteps as we take out the garbage.

Our practice constantly reminds us that everything is worthy of attention. The ant walking across the floor. The piece of fruit you're eating. Each breath. These things are our lives, moment by moment. If we don't notice them, we don't make contact with the full vividness of life.

It is a great, though rather common, mistake to think that the practice just involves sitting. It's wonderful to have a place where you can reliably get calm—if sitting does that for you—but you don't want to create a split between that part of your life and the rest, seeing one as more important than the other. Our practice is nondualistic. Buddha Dharma is world Dharma; world Dharma is Buddha Dharma. Living wholeheartedly involves being fully present in whatever your life is at a particular moment.

One of the most famous examples of wholeheartedness, one of the most frequently told Zen stories attributed to the Buddha, concerns the time when he appeared before a large group of meditators and held up a flower. He was known to be a great teacher, to have a deep teaching, so all the yogis wondered what he could possibly mean by such a gesture. But Maha Kassapa just smiled, experiencing the flower, with no thinking in the way. The Buddha smiled back. That was a great and notable transmission of the teaching, because that monk was fully present to what was there.

The ancient Chinese Zen masters referred to those times when we're not quite present, when we're divided from what's happening—often by thought—as killing life. Sometimes the Buddhist precept against killing is interpreted in that way. We're killing the moments of our life when we're not fully living them, not experiencing them. When we are fully present, we are giving life to life.

That is the real reason that the Zen archer didn't worry about the target. The target is everywhere. When Dogen gave instructions to the cook, he was very clear on this matter. You give the same attention to a soup of wilted greens that you do to a gourmet cream soup. You give the same attention to an ordinary meal that you give to one for visiting dignitaries. And if you are interrupted at the task—even by Manjushri Bodhisattva—you chase him from the kitchen. Your attention is centered on what is before you.

So this simple instruction, which seems to be just about the breath, is really about much more. To be mindful of something—of anything—is an act of generosity. You are giving it life by allowing it into your world. But the greatest benefactor—because you're showing respect to your own life—is you. The real target is the archer.

MOVING INTO THE BODY

In these first two contemplations, though many other things come up, we're studying a basic phenomenon of nature. We see what a deep breath is, when we feel the breath way down in the belly, perhaps even feel subtle breath sensations in other parts of the body, in the back and sides, in the feet and toes, in the hands. We see what a shallow breath is, when it doesn't seem to go much beyond the chest. We see all the subtle gradations in between. We begin to notice how the rest of the body is when we breathe deeply and when we don't, not trying to change any of that, not trying to breathe differently, just seeing how it all works. That moves us rather naturally into the third contemplation.

> 3. One trains oneself: "Sensitive to the whole body, I breathe in. Sensitive to the whole body, I breathe out."

This third contemplation also marks a distinct change. The breath is no longer an exclusive object; it recedes into the background, though it remains a clear and constant aid to presence. In a sense we're examining two bodies, seeing how the body of breath influences the body of flesh and blood. It has a powerful effect. The act of breathing begins our life as we come out of the womb; in our last moment, when we cease breathing, our life is over. It only makes sense that the breath should also have a profound influence on all the moments in between.

As the breath becomes deeper and finer, smoothing out a little—which happens naturally as your continuity of attention develops—we may find that the body becomes more relaxed, and we can sit for longer periods with ease, with fewer problems of physical pain and numbness. The breath becomes pleasant; it is enjoyable just to sit and breathe. The mind, which has been scattered, chasing after bones, begins to settle in on itself. The body, the mind, and the breath begin to coalesce. They each partake of the other, so that it is difficult to distinguish among them.

This isn't a trance, just a wonderful feeling of peace and stability. It doesn't happen just to people who live in the Himalayas or who lived a thousand years ago. Many modern Westerners have already experienced the lawfulness of this process. As we experience this feeling of stability, real vipassana practice begins to be possible.

Pure vipassana practice—this is to give a preview of where things are headed—begins with the thirteenth contemplation, where you see into the nature of the object and see that all things are impermanent. You might from that vantage point go back and study impermanence with the other contemplations, seeing that the breath itself, for instance, arises and passes away.

"I already know that," you might say. Well, you do. And you also don't. There are deeper kinds of knowing, progressively deeper levels, until finally the knowledge becomes internalized. We become so in touch with things that we are the Dharma. That implies a great letting go, of course, which is usually the fruit of endless practice. Two billion times we attach to something, and finally on the two billion and first we don't, because we see that our attachment only makes us suffer and doesn't change things. We become at one with how things are.

Even this early in the practice, as we begin to perceive certain truths—that attention deepens the breathing, deep breathing re-laxes the body—a faith develops that wasn't there before. We need some faith in order to launch a practice and to keep it going until we actually experience the fruits of our efforts. The Buddha is asking in all these teachings that we examine the outcome of practice to see if the teachings are true. Buddhism isn't about beliefs. It's about firsthand knowledge.

THE BODY AS AN OBJECT OF NATURE

This third contemplation opens up a profound subject that has elicited a great deal of commentary through the centuries. The *Anapanasati Sutra* in general is a kind of dharma telegram, ex-tremely concise, which many commentators have elaborated on. It also, as I mentioned before, goes hand in hand with the *Satipat-thana Sutra*, which outlines the Four Foundations of Mindfulness, the first of which is the contemplation of the body. Ultimately, this third contemplation focuses on the true nature of the body.

Many of us identify totally with the body, believing we are

our bodies. That is obviously an extremely strong attitude in our culture, with health-care products, health food stores, exercise studios, tanning salons. Our culture worships young, thin, healthy, beautiful bodies, and most of us (since few of us have such a body, and none of us has one for long) strive after that ideal.

The other side of the coin—and people sometimes alternate between these two states—is revulsion with the body, an utter alienation from it. That might develop as we bulge here and there, start to wrinkle, go gray at the temples. But it is also a prominent feature of the spiritual world, and always has been, reflected in practices that demean and deny the body, trying to act as if—with all it's wants and needs—it doesn't exist.

In a way Buddhism is between these two views; in another way it is beyond either of them. There is no question, according to the Buddha, that the body exists. But it is also true that—except conventionally, and perhaps legally—it isn't yours. In a profound way, we don't own our bodies.

A little simple observation will let us know that the body does just what it wants and that we aren't in control. It tells us when it's hungry, when it's full and doesn't need more food (we don't listen to that very well), when it has to go to the bathroom, when it's tired and needs to sleep. We can ignore these requests, of course, but only at our peril, and we can't ignore them forever. The body is in charge. And no matter how many vitamins we take, how much exercise we do, how perfect our diet is, our body's reaction is finally unpredictable. We don't—to name only the most obvious example—know when it is going to give out on us altogether. Our fate is strangely intertwined with this fragile and unpredictable object known as a body.

The Dharma attitude is not to neglect the body. There's nothing wrong with keeping healthy or looking good, as long as you're not attached to the process. It's rather like the attitude of a cavalry rider to his horse: of course he's going to take care of it. The exploration of the body—undertaken by means of the breath—is an opportunity to examine a marvelous and intricate aspect of nature. It's more intimate than the moon and the stars, or the plants or the animal kingdom, because you're in it. And as you look into it and see its true nature, there is liberation in that seeing.

Take something that we've already noticed: that attention to the breath can relax and condition the body. That in itself is a powerful fact to have seen, and it gives you an indirect way to take care of the body. When you've seen that enough times, again and again, it becomes something you've mastered. You know it, in a way much deeper than just saying it.

SETTLING INTO THE BODY

There are various techniques for moving gracefully from a focus on the breathing to the larger field of the body. One is the way we've already mentioned, which comes about naturally: just pay close attention to the breathing, and as you gradually become stiller, you will begin to notice breath sensations throughout the body. Blockages will work themselves out over time, and you will feel yourself in touch with a field of energy we are calling the whole body.

It is also possible to use a formal, more directed method to enter into the body more systematically. You can begin a given sitting with the breathing, and when you've calmed down a bit, move your attention through the body, focusing on one part after another. Breathing in, breathing out, you notice sensations or their lack in the scalp; breathing in, breathing out, you notice the forehead, then the eyes, the nose, the back of the head, the ears, and so on.

This is not a visualization and doesn't involve thinking. You just experience the sensations in these places. You go into your right eye, for instance, and see what you can feel there. You stay in a place as long as you want, and move your way down through the body, being careful not to lose touch with the breathing.

Once you do that a few times, you can, as a supplementary practice, add reflections on various body parts. You can reflect on your eyes, how precious they are, the fact that many people don't have vision, while you do. You can reflect on all the wonderful things that come in through your eyes. It's a way of no longer taking things for granted. You can do that with every organ and with the whole body. This practice is especially helpful when a meditator is feeling down, when everything seems to be going wrong. Moving through the body can show you all that is right in your life and revitalize your interest in practice.

The idea is not to develop the kind of attachment to the body that we spoke of before but to appreciate this body that has been entrusted to us for a given number of years. It becomes a rich contemplation. Not only do you get to know the body better, but you use the breathing to know something other than breath, an ability that is vital for this sutra. It can lead to increased concentration and decreased attachment, an appreciation without clinging.

The first four contemplations prepare us to enter what are known as the *jhanas*, eight highly concentrated states, each defined by increasing refinement, in which—by becoming more at home in the body, laying to rest any blockages of energy, learning to sit in a stable and comfortable way—we provide an opportunity for the mind to become deeply absorbed. Anyone who has practiced for a while will acknowledge with deep respect the importance of a calm and concentrated mind. Without some degree of serenity and stability, we can't absorb the Buddha's teaching. We are gradually equipping the mind to learn.

In another directed meditation, you pick a region of the body— the pelvis and abdomen, for instance—and see what breath sensations you can feel there. The abdomen, of course, is one of the most common sites for following the breathing, but in this kind of guided meditation you direct your attention to specific spots, the left side, the right, the back, and so on. If you have time, you cover the entire body. Some parts, when you first move into them, may feel blocked or dead, but you don't worry about that. They become enlivened in time. Eventually you find that you can feel subtle breath sensations throughout the body.

All of these exercises have the effect of bringing the mind, the body, and the breath together, so that they form a unity. That is one of the central aims of the third contemplation. When we begin this practice, there is an observer and a process he or she is observing. But in time that boundary—which has been imposed upon us—disappears. Everything is a part of everything else. There is an incredible stillness and calm.

THE BODY'S ULTIMATE FATE

Another way to focus on the body—death awareness—sounds more radical, but it also comes from the *Satipatthana Sutra*. In ancient times, the yogis would actually go to the charnel grounds after someone died and observe the process of decomposition. They would camp there for extended periods of time to observe a single body, but there were many bodies around, and they also might move from one to another, observing the various states of this process.

We can't do that, but the Buddha left behind an extensive series of images detailing what happens. All of these contemplations arouse profound feelings, such as fear and revulsion, so you don't want to try them until you're ready. But the process can be an important one, as you visualize various stages your body will eventually go through. In the charnel grounds, there would be various bones lying around, a leg bone here, a shoulder blade there. That is one of the stages to contemplate. Finally, of course, the bones dissolve and there is just dust. The wind blows away the dust.

That is our ultimate fate. There's no doubt about it.

The point of such contemplations isn't to create a sense of morbidity. It's just to balance out the idealization of the body, because that attitude creates a great deal of suffering. No matter what we hope, the body is going to follow the laws of nature.

I myself have done a great deal of death awareness practice, and found it to be quite wonderful. I worked with Ajahn Suwat and did it continuously during my waking hours for about a month. At first all kinds of things came up: nausea, terror, bitterness, and disappointment. I had worked so hard, done so many things with my life, and this was what was to come of it all. Whatever emotion is aroused by seeing a body in a state of decomposition—resentment, horror, deep sadness—that is what you bring your attention to, the same way you do with the breathing. Little by little, you get more comfortable with this law of nature. You don't even see it as ugly, just a part of the way things are.

One visualization I've done a lot, and introduced to my students, is to picture the skeleton that we will someday be. For some reason, that has always been quite easy for me. I have done walking meditation for hours at a time, picturing myself as a skeleton. It got to a point where I didn't even have to try. It was perfectly obvious. I also did that visualization while sitting, with the breath as a companion. And gradually, as you do that practice, the fact becomes internalized. It sinks into our consciousness that we're someday going to be a skeleton. That knowledge gives us a new relationship with our body.

My teacher was very skillful. I would get good at seeing the decomposed body and he would say, "All right, now recreate it. Make it young and firm and attractive." I'd do that and he'd say, "Now let it go again." We would also go inside the body and see its various constituents, urine, feces, pus, blood. It wasn't just a matter of calling up aversion but of countering the idealization and romanticizing of the body. After all, these unsavory elements are a part of it.

So you don't leave it at aversion. You come back to a place of balance, a natural and healthy relationship to things. There is a body, which is a miraculous process, to be enjoyed in relationship and in all of life. It is also going to die. We want to maintain total fidelity to the law, to the way things actually are.

STAGES OF CALM

At this point, you might be beginning to get an idea of how this sutra works. It is a series of contemplations that you can work your way through systematically. It is also a description of what will happen naturally if you take up the practice of focusing on the breathing. The steps blend into one another. Just as, when the breathing becomes deeper, you'll naturally start to focus on the body, the fourth step also follows out of the third. It isn't something to try for but just to let happen. If you look back, though the steps have merged into one another, you will see that you are actually quite far from the initial instruction.

> 4. One trains oneself: "Calming the whole body, I
> breathe in. Calming the whole body, I breathe out."

In some ways, there is no need to elaborate. The fourth contemplation invites us to explore the realm of concentrated stillness, which has many levels. But the Buddha and some later practitioners left behind some guidelines, some names and demarcation points, to help us understand what is happening. One convenient one—which I've already mentioned—is the *jhanas*, or levels of absorption. The first of these involves a coming together of five factors, which I'd like to sketch out so that you'll see their value to the rest of the practice.

The first two factors will sound familiar. One is *vitakka*, the bringing of attention to an object, which in a way combines the first two qualities of a healthy mind, energy and mindfulness. You develop the ability to aim and bring the mind to a particular object—such as the breath—at will. The second is called *vicara*, or evaluation, the ability to keep the mind interested in an object. First we have to get to the breath, then we have to stay there without constantly slipping off. These two factors work together, and at times they almost fuse. Sometimes, for a given individual, one is stronger than the other. But as the practice progresses, both grow strong.

The next quality is quite dramatic, what is known as *piti*, or rapture. It is an enlivened feeling of strong energy. This might be just a flash, it might appear quite suddenly and be gone. You might not feel it again for months. On the other hand, it might become quite regular. It can permeate the entire body, so that the body feels almost transparent. It feels simultaneously as if there is nothing there and also as if the body is much more than it has ever been before. It is not really a peaceful feeling, though there is some peace in it. It is exciting. We tend to like it, especially as it gets stronger. We want to stay there. Finally—though this sounds hard to believe—it can get to be annoying. There is just not enough peace in it. Sometimes on retreat it goes on for long periods of time. You'd do anything not to be so excited.

Past rapture you come to *sukha*, or pleasure. This is much more fulfilling but also more dangerous. The stimulating aspects of rapture, the giddy ecstasy of it, fall away. You come to a great peace and calm.

The ancients developed an image to distinguish these states. They said that if a person were in a desert and had gone for a long time without water, then finally found some water and knew that his terrible thirst was about to be relieved, that would be piti. But when he drank the water and felt relief, felt content, that would be sukha.

Piti and sukha—sometimes referred to as higher kinds of happiness—are not the end of the journey by any means, but they are quite significant. If they should happen to arise for you, at this or any other stage of your practice, the instruction is just to be mindful of them, the same as with anything else. You'll see that they have varying degrees of subtlety and intensity and are the natural fruit of a concentrated mind.

That connection gives you much more motivation to practice. If you can get intimate with the state of sukha, so that it is very real to you, it becomes much easier to get back to it. You just sit down, notice a few breaths, and you're there. That isn't an ability that develops quickly, but it may develop over time, through practice.

This kind of stillness and happiness leads to the fifth factor, *ekaggata*, or one-pointedness, which is often used as a synonym for concentration (*samadhi*), characterized by nondistraction, nonwavering. The mind becomes extremely focused, like a laser beam, like a lens that marshals the rays of the sun. It becomes supple and flexible as well as steady, making it much more fit to look at itself, to develop the insight that will lead to liberation.

There are other benefits to these states as well. The peace and happiness that I'm describing come from within; they don't have to do with whether you're healthy or sick, young or old, rich or poor. You're no longer so vulnerable to how the world treats you. You're not like a beggar—which is the way we are much of the time—looking into people's eyes to see that you're all right.

That isn't to say that these states should cut us off from the world. We're just less dependent on external conditions. We have a source of fulfillment inside us. So we still need a job, we still have relationships, we still face the problems that anyone faces in life. But a certain desperate quality is missing. We have a quiet ally in the fact that the mind can become stable and concentrated. And our faith in the practice is strengthened by such stability. We are keen to practice even more.

Unfortunately, this same ability can be a trap. I have never seen anyone who experienced sukha who didn't become attached to it, and attachment—even to an advantageous state —is a problem. It does tend to remove you from the world, for one thing; you just want to get off and sit. You're staying out of trouble—not strengthening your negative states—and you are strengthening mindfulness, our greatest ally, but you're not doing much of anything else.

At this point it's helpful to have a friend—probably a teacher—who has already been there, who can say, "This is all very nice, but there's no insight in it." Our first reaction, of course, is to say, "I don't need insight if I feel like this."

The problem is that you don't always feel like that. One of the best ways to be weaned from this blissed-out state is to see that it, too, arises and passes away. It can become the source of real suffering, not only because it ends, but because we keep struggling to get back to it. No matter how valuable, it is ultimately limited. The practice is not just about calm, though calm is a vital step along the way.

At its worst—confined to the joys of a concentrated mind—meditation becomes a sanctuary that people drop into to get away from things, instead of a means to lead them into a fuller life. They don't work on their demons, so the demons remain strong. Such people are still deluded, just very calm in their delusion. They are calm fools.

The point is to use that calm mind, even the joy that comes from it, to look deeply into ourselves. That is the heart of vipassana practice. It starts off being awareness of an object, like the breath or the body, and winds up being awareness itself. Our direction is always toward the knowing.

2

Breathing with Feelings

The first four contemplations of the *Anapanasati Sutra* involve the long process of acquiring a seat, stabilizing the mind, and familiarizing ourselves with the body. We begin by simply bringing attention to the breathing, and different qualities of the breath soon become evident. We notice that no two breaths are the same. Over time, the quality of our breathing becomes deeper and finer. The breath becomes more vivid and more easily noticeable throughout the entire body. Sustained attention changes the breath and brings the body and mind along with it. The breath is a vital conditioner of the body.

The body, mind, and breath become one, and you are able to sit for longer periods of time without pain or discomfort. You begin to resemble the tree we mentioned earlier, whose deep roots enable it to weather powerful storms. Your deep roots are the stability of your sitting posture. You may be able to face difficult emotional storms for the first time in your life.

It is important to emphasize that this process unfolds in different ways for different people, that it generally takes place over a long period of time, and that for most of us it is the fruit of a great deal of sitting.

But at some point, having developed a certain serenity, we shift the focus from calming practice to one of inquiry. We sit awake and alert, with keen interest. That shift in focus might well come about at this point in the process, when we move from the contemplation of the body to that of the feelings, the sensations that we experience through the six senses (as mentioned before, Buddhist psychology regards the mind as one of the senses).

So if the fifth and sixth contemplations sound familiar—since we've just gone over these feelings—there is nevertheless a subtle shift in emphasis. In the past we noticed weaker and less-developed stages of these mind states. Now they are much more vivid and stable, and we begin to look into them as specific contemplations.

>   5. One trains oneself: "Sensitive to rapture, I breathe
>   in. Sensitive to rapture, I breathe out."
>   6. One trains oneself: "Sensitive to pleasure, I breathe
>   in. Sensitive to pleasure, I breathe out."

It is obvious that the Buddha considers these states to be normal fruits of the meditation process. In his second set of four contemplations, all of which involve the feelings, these are the first two he mentions.

Rapture can be extremely intense, but it doesn't have to be. It can be heavy or light, coarse or fine. It grows out of calm serene breathing and itself makes the breathing calmer. But once it arises—in this part of the practice—it becomes the object of contemplation. It moves to the foreground, while the body and breath move to the back. Rapture, like the breath, is a whole world.

As we've said, it can give a substantial boost to the practice. It is tangible evidence that something is happening. You no longer have to trust so much in the teacher or the teaching; the practice becomes its own reward. We have all experienced plenty of pain and suffering in our lives, and rapture seems to be a balm for that.

It can also seem an accomplishment, and in that way be a problem. We're so tied to the progressive scheme of accomplishment—B.A., M.A., Ph.D.—that we begin to build that into the practice. We had this much rapture; now we want that much. We want to have more. It gets to be like food, money, sex, power. It can lead to real suffering. Trungpa Rinpoche was onto something when he spoke of spiritual materialism, where Dharma practice is used to enhance one's sense of self.

The same thing can happen with sukha—pleasure—which grows out of rapture and becomes a deep state of stillness and peace. Sometimes it exists while the rapture is going on. They might intermingle, with rapture dominating. But as the mind grows steady, the rapture seems to lose some of its energy, and what emerges is a deep peace. It is within that stillness that you can begin to do insight work, which is very hard to do within the dynamic intensity of rapture.

Because it is so peaceful, sukha is especially seductive. It seems to be nirvana, or at least what we've imagined nirvana to be. We'd like to live in that calm for the rest of our lives. But it isn't nirvana; it's a state that—like everything else—comes and goes. What wisdom ultimately tells us is that it is impermanent, unsatisfactory, and lacking in substance.

Sometimes it seems that the Buddha is always raining on our parade, trying to stamp out all the happiness we have. Actually, he is trying to end our suffering. He is speaking from the vantage point of awakening and can see that rapture and happiness emerge from a given set of conditions, from a calm that we develop in meditation. But—as any meditator can tell you—meditative states are ephemeral, and can be especially so when you're trying to hold on to them. Rapture and happiness, however deep they may seem, are not ultimately fulfilling. They have a certain existential loneliness to them, a trace of me and mine. They disappear when the conditions that produced them end. And when they do, if we're attached to them, we suffer.

That isn't to say you shouldn't enjoy these states when they arise. If you find some calm and peace in your sitting, soak in it. Let it work on you. You may discover an inner strength you didn't know you had and be less compulsive about searching for happiness outside of yourself.

FLOWERS WILT

In many Buddhist temples, monasteries, and meditation centers, flower arrangements are part of the decor, and they not only beautify the setting but also offer a valuable teaching. On the first day the flowers are fresh and beautiful, vibrant and fragrant, and it heartens us to see them. On the second day, perhaps, they have lost some of their fragrance. Soon they begin to droop, the petals start to fall, and before long—despite our admiration—they go and die on us.

Do we conclude from that experience that we'll never enjoy a flower again, because they always wither and die and disappoint us? Or do we enjoy them while they're here, take them in fully when we're with them, and when they're gone, experience a moment's sadness and move on? It's the same with any human experience. It's the same with rapture and happiness.

As we begin to look at these states, we not only see that they are impermanent (see it in a deep way, not in the intellectual sense that we have always known it), we also see what we do with that, the longing we have for them to stay, our chasing after them once they're gone, our dissatisfaction with other states that don't seem as good. Much of our life is spent bouncing around that way, running toward some things and away from others.

We also see how these states nourish a sense of me and mine: this is my rapture, I am so happy in this moment, I have such a wonderful practice, I love being a Buddhist (as long as I'm experiencing rapture). It goes on and on. A new kind of attachment appears, to extremely attractive meditation states. If we grasp on to them the way we do food, sex, money, power, fame, we get burned in exactly the same way.

Weariness may also begin to set in—this is actually a healthy sign—at the enormous burden of working for the ego. Most of us, before we see this, don't realize why we're so tired, or even how tired we are. But we spend our whole day nourishing the ego, being told by it what to do, maintaining and protecting it, being wounded in it. It's exhausting.

All the Buddha's teachings, it has been said, can be reduced to one: Under no circumstances attach to anything as me or mine. It isn't that we shouldn't experience rapture or happiness but that we have to be careful not to attach to them. When we do, we need to see that fact with mindfulness. Such seeing protects us.

The challenge becomes: Can we experience rapture and happiness fully, then allow them to go when they're over? Can we allow the laws of nature to work? They're going to work anyway, whether we allow them or not. But can we surrender to them, the same way we surrendered to the breathing?

Clearly at this point we've switched to vipassana practice, to the insights that comprise wisdom. We're not just calming and concentrating; we're looking at the nature of the object, even if the object is calmness itself. We see that we've taken something insubstantial and imbued it with a core; we've regarded it as something we can hold on to; we've decided it belongs to us. When we look more carefully, we see that all these suppositions are illusory. We have to let these impermanent states come and go.

The main door into all Buddhist work is this one of impermanence, or emptiness. That doesn't mean—as we sometimes mistakenly think—that things aren't here, but that they aren't here in the way we imagine they are. We ourselves are not solid in that way; we create notions of who we are out of memory and various ideals, then exhaust ourselves trying to maintain that image. When the time finally comes that we can let go of that, it's a tremendous relief. And we have abundant energy for other things.

But these states of rapture and pleasure—though impermanent—can be extremely valuable. As you get more and more familiar with them, you can drop into them almost at will. In my own life, I have in recent years had to care for aging and dying parents. I've had to learn about powers of attorney and look into various kinds of care for the aging; I've spent hours and days in a bewildering maze that many of you must be familiar with.

I am the kind of person—as my friends will tell you—who has frequently avoided any activity that required the filling out of forms. Now I had to fill out dozens of forms. It sometimes felt oppressive, and I found myself barely paying attention, hurrying to end the process. But in the midst of that, if I could just get off and drop into that place of stillness for a while—not so much vipassana practice, just simple samadhi, following the breath—I emerged refreshed, able to go on with a series of tasks that I didn't much care to undertake. I saw the value of these states of calm as I almost never had.

NOW CLEAN THE TOILET

All this can sound rather esoteric—rapture, bliss, impermanence, lack of self—and it is important not to let the practice become a cluster of words up in your head. You don't want to create an image of yourself, a stone Buddha like those you see around various centers, always sitting in the lotus posture and discerning marvelous wisdom. The whole point of a book like this, of retreats and classes, of sitting practice itself, is for you to take the practice into everyday life, to practice moment by moment. You can learn everything I've said just as well by cleaning the toilet.

When I teach classes, I always speak for a while about daily life, trying to get students to talk about how they take the practice into the outside world. It isn't easy, either to do that or to talk about it. It's much easier to talk about the ethereal theories of Buddhism, especially for the highly educated and intellectual people attracted to meditation in the West.

On retreats at the Insight Meditation Society, we have a work period every day, and every meditator has a job, not just because it helps maintain the place (though it does), but in order to make a vital connection about the practice. Most days in your life you work a lot and sit in meditation a little. On retreat you sit a lot and work a little. How you take your practice into that work period says a lot about how you will take it back to your life.

Some of the jobs are not especially attractive. We have a great many toilets, and all of them need to be cleaned, preferably by a corporate head, or at least a distinguished professor. Actually, I shouldn't make fun of those people. Some of the most experienced and efficient housewives hate to clean the toilet.

But the practice is just to do it. You're on your knees, cleaning the toilet bowl, and maybe you have a spray bottle and some kind of long-handled scrubber. You hear the sounds that the sprayer makes and that the scrubber makes against the top of the bowl; you see the spots you missed, the dirt that is hard to get off. And when you find yourself thinking about the ball game the other night, or your upcoming vacation, you come back (without blame) to the toilet bowl.

You think about how gross this is, how bad it smells, how you'd like to get someone—anyone!—else to do it. You see your aversion and come back to the toilet bowl—not trying to be a perfect toilet scrubber, just the one you are—feeling your muscles cringe, your stomach contract, whatever. This is your life, in this moment. It's not something romantic, like confronting fear. It's confronting a dirty smelly toilet.

One of the things you're likely to run into head-on is the image you've created for yourself. Why am *I* cleaning the toilet? (Or, aren't I a wonderful Buddhist to be cleaning the toilet so mindfully?) But you will also find, if you can be with the activity fully, even for a few moments, that there is a certain joy to it, a certain delight. The joy comes as you begin to learn how to weaken the power of me and mine. You're not feeling that old weariness, the incredible weight of supporting the ego in all its glory.

No one can be with the present task all the time, but the more you can, the more wonderful it is. It's Dharma practice—even cleaning the toilet—because you've begun to touch your true nature, where me and mine don't exist. You're starting to penetrate a level of reality that is just waiting to be enjoyed, waiting to be lived.

One famous answer to the question, "What is enlightenment?" was a simple one, "Eating rice. Drinking tea." Sounds easy. Where's the nearest Chinese restaurant? But that answer was referring to action without any sense of separation, where you totally leave behind the deeply conditioned tendency to engage in selfing. The enlightened mind displays its nature in action.

Enlightenment is beyond the connection to me and mine; it's past the illusion that you know who you are. In our world it is considered advantageous to have a positive self-image, but the wisdom of Buddhism is to let go of images altogether. There is a great deal of suffering in self-esteem. It's nice when it's around, but it comes and goes, utterly out of our control. This practice is headed in the direction of letting go of everything you think you are. Then you're doing the same things other people are—eating rice and drinking tea—but you're beginning to get a taste of what it is like to be free and clear, wholehearted and effortless.

So ordinary life is extremely important. After all, most of us are not monks or nuns in a monastery devoted to meditation. Most of our lives are spent in ordinary activity. But if you take that as a part of your practice—not inferior to monastic life and not superior—it can be extremely rich. As you gradually stop doing things for the sake of the image you have of yourself, you arrive finally at clarity and real compassion. It is possible to cultivate compassion from the outside, by performing loving actions, but the best way is to penetrate to this inner clarity. When you do, you'll find that all the compassion you could want is starting to become available to you.

THE LARGER WORLD OF FEELINGS

Feelings, or *vendana*, are extremely important in the Buddhist scheme of things. At one point the Buddha says that all things converge on feelings. He was not using the word in its contemporary sense, where it is more or less synonymous with emotions. Emotions come later in the Buddhist scheme. It is actually of great practical significance to realize this distinction. The term *feelings*—sometimes called sensations—refers to everything that comes in through the sense doors, including the mind.

When I teach beginner classes at the Cambridge Insight Meditation Center, students are often extremely sensitive to sounds. They're new to meditation, expecting an experience of peace and quiet, and we're located on a busy street in the middle of the city. Sounds come in our windows just as they do for everyone else. Trucks roar by, horns honk. On the other hand, we often hear birds chirping, squirrels chattering.

The meditation hall at the center is not far from the kitchen, and sometimes elaborate and delicious meals are being prepared during a sitting. The aromas waft into the hall and give us a preview of things to come.

With every one of these sense objects, there is an immediate and spontaneous feeling that is either pleasant, unpleasant, or neutral. The scent of vegetable curry drifting through the vents, the sound of a mockingbird going through his morning performance: pleasant. A cement mixer groaning by: unpleasant. The sound of crickets, which goes on all day in the summer: neutral. We don't necessarily notice these feelings—that's part of the problem—but they do take place. Moment by moment, all day long.

Emotions arise because you are not mindful of the feelings. You smell something pleasant and think, "Ah, vegetable curry. I wonder when this sitting is going to end. I can't wait. I do hope they made enough." An elaborate mental state can build up very rapidly. You feel a throb in your leg and think, "Oh, my God. What if it gets worse? What if I have to run out of here like an idiot? Why did I ever come to this retreat? Why did I take up meditation in the first place?"

So clear feeling, that initial moment, is followed almost immediately by attachment, aversion, or boredom. Thoughts—from the mind, the sixth sense—have a flavor too, pleasant, unpleasant, or neutral. We can use the breathing to help us watch the mind in the same way that we're mindful of the body. And thoughts, if we don't watch them, have a way of really getting out of hand, leading to all kinds of mental states—terror, deep sadness, lust, fierce anger, strong craving—and the often destructive actions that come out of them.

In the Buddhist scheme of things, feelings make the world go round. We spend our whole lives trying to pile up good feelings and avoid bad ones; in the face of neutral feelings we tend to space out with thoughts and fantasies. Probably you even opened this book in the hope of having some good feelings.

The problem is that we become slaves to this process. We don't look closely at the feelings that stimulate our reactions; they elaborate themselves into moods, emotions, and a sense of self, which sometimes results in unskillful actions. You grab the person who makes you feel good, kill the one who makes you feel bad. All of the areas that give human beings problems—sex, money, power, drugs, ethnic strife, war—have their source in feelings.

The Buddha saw feelings as the weak link in this chain. If we can catch them at their source, if we can skillfully see them, we can liberate ourselves from unnecessary suffering. We can short-circuit a process that leads to all kinds of human misery.

WHEN THE STUDENT IS READY, THE TEACHER BITES

Some years ago, my first Buddhist teacher got permission for me to do a retreat in Korea that is usually only attended by monks. I was the only layperson there, an American at that, and we took a vow not to move while sitting. (At our center, we ask just that meditators keep movement to a minimum, and to change posture mindfully if they decide to do so. That is a valuable way to practice, but it is also instructive not to move at all.) There was a great deal of ego involved. I felt as if I were sitting there holding the flag. The official American meditator of the Olympic games.

At the beginning of one morning sitting, after the first minute or so, I was bitten by a mosquito. This is a rather ordinary event, but it marked a major turning point in my practice. I am actually deeply grateful to that Korean mosquito. She was just doing her job, of course. She was being a mosquito. But the bite really started to itch. I didn't think I could stand it. There I sat, with fifty-eight minutes between me and the opportunity to scratch.

Right practice, of course, was just to feel the sensation. Forget about mosquitoes, the nature of insect bites, the word *itch*. Just feel exactly what the sensation is on your skin at that moment. The breath is very helpful in that regard. It helps you stay with the object; it nourishes your mindfulness; it cuts down on unnecessary thinking. You can also become absorbed in the breath to take your mind off the powerful urge to scratch.

It's quite varied, this thing we call a mosquito bite: If you look closely, you see that the itch isn't one feeling but a whole host of feelings, coming and going. It's not solid; it's a process. It grows more intense, then less so, disappears altogether for a few seconds, returns with a vengeance.

Sustained awareness perceives this truth; without awareness, it's just a solid sheet of itch. Awareness also sees that the itch is impersonal. It comes from nowhere, goes to nowhere. You don't own it, and it isn't you. It's a phenomenon of the natural world. You're a part of that natural world. It begins to lose its power when you see what it really is.

But if you lose your mindfulness for even a second, all kinds of thoughts rush in: "Who made this rule about not moving anyway? Who are *they* to tell *me* not to move. I hate this practice. I hate this country. I'm just going to go ahead and scratch. They'll have to find a way to deal with it. . . ."

Those thoughts kept rushing in for me—it was a difficult morning—and at some point I had a major realization. I was a highly educated man, had been a college professor; I'd read a great many books, even Dharma books, but I was making this itch into one of the worst catastrophes in human history. If someone had said, "It could be worse. You could be in a Stalinist labor camp," I would have said, "What do you mean? This is worse than any torture Stalin inflicted." My mind had become that deluded, all from—to say the least—a rather trivial stimulus. Imagine what it would have done with a more serious problem.

If you go back to the original feeling, as I did when I was mindful, it still isn't pleasant: nobody wants to itch. But you eliminate an enormous amount of suffering by concentrating on the suffering that is actually present instead of creating more with your thinking. It is the difference between discomfort and torment.

That is a good, if trivial, example of aversion. I have an even more humiliating one of craving. I have always had a great love for anything Indian. The Buddha's teaching comes from India, and I began inner work with yoga, which also originated in that country. I've benefited a great deal from Indian culture.

I also love the taste of Indian food, but, unfortunately, it doesn't agree with me. Years ago I would go through a repeating cycle of taking great enjoyment from an Indian meal, and then an hour later being extremely uncomfortable. "That's it," I'd think. "I'm never going to that restaurant again." A week later somebody would ask me to dinner, and I'd say, "Indian food? Sure. I love it."

You know what will happen if you eat that food, but the craving keeps growing until you say, "I don't care what happens. I've just got to have that taste." Fine. But that is the same decision people make with all kinds of harmful behavior: overeating, drinking, drug use, sexual misconduct. The list could go on and on.

Everything begins with feelings, all the difficult mind states that people get themselves into. The closer you are able to get to that original sensation, the more clearly you can see it.

Start small. Liberate yourself from mosquito bites and see where that might lead.

FEELINGS AND THE MIND

In my translation of the seventh contemplation, the term *mental processes* refers to two things: feelings, which we've been discussing; and perceptions, the labels that the mind gives to its experiences. The labels include, in particular, "me" and "mine."

> 7. One trains oneself: "Sensitive to mental processes, I breathe in. Sensitive to mental processes, I breathe out."

We spoke earlier about the way that the breath conditions the body, that just by bringing attention to the breathing, you make it deeper and smoother, and that quality of the breath in turn relaxes the body, leading to feelings of rapture and peace. In the same way, feelings condition the mind. Rapture, for instance, strongly conditions the thoughts you might have.

This contemplation focuses on a solid lawful relationship. Our feelings condition the way the mind behaves. Mindfulness can alter that connection somewhat, by short-circuiting the process. The connection is particularly operative in the case of what we call unwise or blind feeling, where no mindfulness is operating.

If the feelings are pleasant, we want to hold on to them. We do that with a clinging that can itself become painful; we are clinging to pleasure and thereby feeling pain. If the feelings disappear, we hold on by means of memory, dreaming about the good feeling we had last week instead of noticing what we're feeling now.

If the feelings are unpleasant, we want to get rid of them. We're sitting with a pain in our leg, so we change our posture. We change it again and again, seeking a totally comfortable posture. (That's why the practice of sitting still is so valuable. It eliminates our usual reactions, so we observe the movement of the mind.) If it gets bad enough, we leave the room, leave the center, give up meditation altogether, all because of a pain in our leg.

And if the feelings are neutral, we have a tendency to get bored, project, start having fantasies. There's no telling where that process will lead.

Needless to say, a wide variety of actions emerge from these feelings. Pursuing pleasant feelings, we eat something, drink something, take some drug, have sex. Then we have to deal with the aftermath. We also steal as a result of this kind of craving, and extort, and cheat. And in search of the good feeling of accomplishment, people spend their whole lives pushing themselves in their work, not noticing the abundant and beautiful world around them.

Violent acts often result from pushing away bad feeling, everything from abusive language to physical abuse to rape, murder, even—at a larger level—war. So many of the horrible things that human beings do to each other. And neutral feelings stimulate boredom. Think of all the bizarre things people do when they're bored.

Really, these sixteen contemplations concern the age-old adage that the ancient Greeks used: Know thyself. They involve, not the vague theorizing about the human animal that philosophers often engage in, but self-knowledge in an extremely down-to-earth, practical way, in this very moment. How the breathing is, how the body is. What the feelings are. Ultimately, how the mind is. It's a gradual progression toward greater subtlety. One thing leads to another.

A major part of our problem is that we identify with our feelings and the mind states they produce. I'm a miserable person. An angry person. A calm person. This is where the labeling of feelings comes in. When we examine ourselves with mindfulness, moment by moment, we see what a vast thing a human being actually is, and we see that all these states are not us, just passing phenomena. It makes no more sense to say that I'm an anxious person than it does to say that I'm a mosquito bite. It was the bite, after all, that produced the anxiety. If we stay with our feelings moment by moment, we're able to take a larger perspective.

This kind of focus on feelings can be helpful in extremely complex problems. One of the most vivid examples that comes to mind is that of a seventeen-year-old boy who was the child of a couple at our center in Cambridge. He was having a great deal of trouble in school, and the family suspected he might have a learning disability, but they had him tested and found him to be perfectly all right. He was obviously quite intelligent. That left them stumped. They asked if I thought the vipassana perspective could be of any help.

I'm certainly no expert on learning disabilities. But I sat down with this young man and asked him what the process of studying was like. He said he'd be reading his math textbook and would come to a place where he couldn't grasp the symbols in front of him. The anxiety that arose at that point was terrific. He was from an academic family, knew the hopes his parents had for him. His thoughts would take off from his anxiety, branding him stupid, a failure, a disgrace to the family. He'd quit studying and dread the thought of coming back.

You can imagine what I told him. After a while the wisdom in this practice is glaringly obvious. The problem wasn't that he didn't understand the symbols. It was the feeling that arose out of the situation, and what his mind did with it. What he had to do was experience that feeling and acknowledge that it wasn't him. And watch it, as he gave it that close attention, change and eventually pass away. If he could handle the feeling, he'd usually be able to understand the material eventually. It all became more workable.

That is why it is so helpful to be mindful: sharp, alert, and sensitive. You catch the whole process earlier, when it is much easier to stop. You won't avoid unpleasant feelings. The Buddha himself experienced them. He is said to have suffered dysentery on the last day of his life, and that can't have been too pleasant. But you just experience these feelings; they don't proliferate into mind states. And that makes all the difference.

ONE WITH THE FEELING

In a way, in this practice, the instructions just keep repeating. In another way they keep changing, because the practice grows deeper and they seem different. Now might be a good time to, in a sense, repeat the instructions, applying them in this new way. At first I spoke only of the breathing. Now the object of attention is also feeling. The process I'm describing is worth coming back to again and again, because it is one way in which the practice can really be helpful.

We're learning to pay attention to what is, to give full attention to what is. As I write, there is a small knot at the top of my stomach. I focus on the feeling: a slight pressure, a full feeling, at the top of the stomach. Perhaps there is some vivid feeling in your body that you can focus on as you read this.

That feeling of pressure becomes the object of my attention. I don't pull back from it. It is getting more intense, but I don't detach from it; I come in close and touch it. There's the feeling in my stomach, which is unpleasant; there's mindfulness, which is able to turn to it; and there's conscious breathing, which nourishes the mindfulness and keeps it on course. Part of the way it does that is to cut down on unnecessary thinking. When you're perfectly attentive, there's no thinking. This attention has nothing to do with concepts.

We go in and out of that, of course; we lose it for a moment and thoughts come rushing in, labels and interpretations, analytic conclusions, then it all subsides and we're concentrated again. We're not trying to banish thinking. We're not at war with anything. But as the attention becomes naturally stronger, it halts the movement of thought.

So we're fully attentive again, with our whole being. Everything is focused on that sensation. We're not trying to add to it, subtract from it, make it feel better, change it in any way. We try to experience it with no separation whatsover. Even being a self-conscious observer is separation. We have spent years being egocentric and divided. It feels as if there's me and there's a pain in my stomach, as if the pain is an alien thing, attacking me. There's a struggle going on; I want to get rid of it. A great deal of energy goes into that struggle.

Instead of fighting the feeling, or turning away from it, we're learning—gradually, through practice—to turn toward it. As the art of observation matures, observation is certainly taking place, but no one is doing it. You might think, "That's crazy. *I*'m doing it." But that "I" is just a notion. This sense of "I" serves to distance and separate us from the unwanted. We can learn to welcome the unwanted, simply because it is there and is our life in that moment.

In the beginning of the book, it was the breathing that we turned to. Now it is a pain in the stomach. Eventually it might be a much more complex and threatening process, loneliness or anger or fear, states that are really unwanted. We come to see that there is great value in the enormous, unwanted energy tied up in fear and anger. There is a saying, "Big clay, big Buddha. Small clay, small Buddha." To be liberated from this pain in my stomach—to be able to feel it fully and have it be all right—might be a small Buddha. To do the same thing with fear or anger would be a big one.

You don't try to make liberation happen. That would be the action of me or mine, the self-conscious practitioner. Real meditation begins when the meditator dies. The meditator is still alive when he's trying to get somewhere, to be a Buddha, attain nirvana. All of that is natural at first; of course you want to get somewhere: that's why you took up the practice. But as time goes on, in a natural way, you see that such goals are just more notions and that they cause suffering. As the practice continues, there is such a surrender to the object that there's nothing outside the observation.

We don't *become* one with the object. We already *are* one with it. We're separated only by our self-consciousness, which is our problem with everything, not just a pain in our stomach. As we let go of self-consciousness, we become what we really are. I am at this moment the pain in my stomach and the breathing and the sound of a machine thudding in the distance and the squawking of a bird outside my window and my pen moving across the page; you are your eyes taking in these words and whatever else is going on for you. The next moment we're something else. And that's what we are all day long, whatever is happening.

If your feeling just now is, "I don't know what you're talking about," don't worry about it. I'm describing the direction in which the practice is headed. As samadhi becomes stronger, there's less self-consciousness about what you're doing, about being a meditator. There is no you meditating. There is just meditation.

DON'T TRY

The first time I ever experienced the absence of the meditator, I was on a retreat and having a hard time. My mind was all over the place, thinking about everything. I was struggling to concentrate and calm the mind. Then the bell rang; the sitting was over; I stopped trying. And it happened: I let everything be as it was and just felt it. It was a wonderful feeling.

I'd learned something extremely important in that moment. I'd seen the wisdom of not trying.

There is a basic mystery to this energy of mindfulness. It has no color, no weight. You can't grab hold of it. But it is extremely powerful, all on its own. When you direct it at a painful or unpleasant feeling, there is a transformation. It is like the ancient idea of alchemy, which was said to transform a base metal into gold. The base metal is our craving, aversion, or confusion. The fire is our attention. The hermetically sealed container is concentration. The gold that comes out of it is liberation. Sometimes the unpleasant feelings become neutral, or pleasant, though that isn't the point. You're not trying to change anything. Mindfulness itself is a subtle energy with transformative power.

Awareness is an energy that transforms anything it comes in contact with. It doesn't work if you *try* to transform anything, because then you're divided. Part of you is in an imaginary future. You have a goal—to get rid of the pain—which is the same old thing we've been doing all our lives. But when you fully experience the feeling in an undivided way, without any wish to add or subtract, something happens.

It is like the story of the young man who had spent seven months in a Zen monastery in Japan and finally decided to leave. It was a Rinzai monastery, so his only real contact with his teacher had been the interviews about his koan, which he had never been able to answer. But as he was leaving, the teacher said, "Is there anything you want to ask me?" The young man thought for a moment, then said, "Will my knees always hurt when I do sitting meditation?" The teacher smiled. "Yes," he said. "But after a while you won't care."

At first when you start to practice, it's very hard to concentrate on unpleasant feelings. The mind wanders. It fantasizes. It thinks up ways to end the suffering. Concentration is beginning to develop when the mind is unwavering in its ability to stay with an unpleasant feeling. You can't force the attention to do that. Forcing doesn't work. The experience is more one of softening into the unpleasant feeling. You soften and the attention is able to rest on the feeling.

CALMING THE MENTAL PROCESSES

As with the other contemplations, the eighth follows naturally out of the seventh. You don't try to do it, it just happens.

> 8. One trains oneself: "Calming mental processes,
> I breathe in. Calming mental processes, I breathe
> out."

This contemplation leads to a great deal of misunderstanding. It reflects, in fact, a misunderstanding that people have about

69

Buddhism in general, that Buddhists are quiet passive people who wear warm smiles and never feel much of anything.

Students ask if this contemplation means that they will not feel things as intensely as in the past. It doesn't. Who would want that, not to feel life as intensely as other people? Actually, a mindful person feels things more fully, feels sensations in all their exquisite detail, but without being tyrannized by them. Such a person doesn't identify with the sensations, and they don't lead to selfing. The act of feeling things fully, mindfully, is what keeps them from conditioning the mind.

A huge amount of fear, anxiety, apprehension, is stimulated by thought itself. You might be doing fairly well in the moment, relatively healthy, well rested, well fed. But some feeling disturbs that state—as with that seventeen-year-old boy who felt the unpleasant feeling of not understanding symbols—and then thought begins (I'm stupid, I'm a failure, my parents won't love me). Pretty soon it's as if those things have already happened, even though you're the same healthy, well-fed and rested person as before. It's as if we have already been rejected, have already failed in life.

The same thing happens with pleasant thoughts, but we don't perceive that as suffering. Someone pays us a compliment or gives us a little attention, and we feel a glow from that, a warmth. Soon—in our head—we see a romance developing, a whirlwind courtship, followed by a lavish wedding and a honeymoon in Acapulco. There we sit, sipping margaritas on the beach. Finally, that feeling does lead to suffering, when we come down and notice we're in Cambridge in the middle of winter. And the person in question hasn't actually called.

So all kinds of feelings lead to suffering. But we probably have more trouble with unpleasant feelings, because the skillful way to handle them is so counterintuitive. It seems natural to avoid bad feelings. We've spent our whole lives doing that, and our well-meaning parents—who didn't want us to suffer—encouraged us. "Don't be sad. Let's see a smile on that face. Have a cookie!"

The spiritual path seems to be creating more suffering, because it asks you to experience suffering that you used to avoid. Actually, of course, this paying attention is the way out of suffering.

Our instinct is to do almost anything else. Take the feeling of fear, for instance, which is behind many of our unpleasant feelings. It was probably behind most of the problems of that seventeen-year-old boy. One thing we commonly do is deny it. We're experts at that. Many of us deny fear so well that we're not even aware of feeling it. We no longer recognize it.

We also repress it. We escape from it. We find countless ways to do that. One of the major ones—especially for intellectual types—is to theorize about it. "This is what Freud said about fear. Jung. Here's what the Buddha said." But verbal explanations never free us. They are just—as one teacher said—the finger pointing at the moon. You've got to experience the moon. Especially in meditation interviews, people talk intelligently about their fear, as if they know a great deal about it. But what they know is in the realm of satisfying explanations. They've done very little being aware of the energy of fear as it is actually happening.

Instead, what probably happened was that they drowned in their fear. They got caught up in it, the same way—in meditation—we get caught up in thought and drift away from the breath. Afterward, they were able to reconstruct it, see exactly what happened, and speak intelligently about it. But they hadn't been especially present when it happened.

The meditation masters in ancient India often used a metaphor for fear: a dimly lit room where you see a rope and think it's a snake. Much of our fear is like that. It begins with a misperception, then one frightened thought leads to another. The practice involves beginning to see clearly: a rope is a rope and a snake is a snake. If there really is a snake in the room, fear may be an appropriate response. But much of our fear is about ropes, which we have never gotten to know, so we spend our lives coping, running, concealing, denying, concocting elaborate verbal explanations.

Our usual reaction to fear is to create a battlefield. Our fear is at war with our tremendous yearning to be free from it, and the site of the battle is the mind and body in which the process is taking place. We tie ourselves into knots, turn ourselves inside out, fighting that battle. The attitude of practice is to open the process up, to see that it's all part of us: the fear, the yearning to be free of it, the mind and body, the mindfulness observing them, the conscious breathing that nourishes the mindfulness. We sit there with all of that, all one thing.

It may be that at first, with a strong feeling like fear, you'll mostly be watching your means of escape. That can be valuable too. You see yourself denying, repressing, explaining, running away, fantasizing. You might watch these things again and again, until finally—because you're not buying into them—the mind gets tired. Then one day—and you can't force this—fear comes up and attention meets it, becomes one with it, allows the fear to blossom, which was what the fear wanted all along.

"The world is many blooming flowers in a blooming universe," one Zen teacher used to say. That sounds syrupy and sentimental, but he didn't mean it that way. He was including fear, anger, loneliness, hatred, and envy among his blossoming flowers. That is what all phenomena want, just to be allowed to arise and pass away in their own time.

It is when we prevent that blossoming—by ignoring or repressing it—that fear hangs around, dragging us down, because we are expending so much energy holding it off. If we let it blossom, it has its life and departs. Then we have all the energy we would have used to escape or combat it. We also have the energy of the fear itself. There is a great gain in energy when we let things happen.

The ground of fearlessness is fear. In order to become fearless, you have to stand in the middle of your fear. We shouldn't trust any fearlessness that doesn't have that as its basis. The beginning of that is to see your fear and admit to it, acknowledge that you're afraid, then have the immense courage—and humility—to study it. It can be a long process.

Often with our practice, as with much in life, we get trapped into thinking it should always be a warm fulfilling experience. You should be experiencing rapture or happiness all the time, with a warm glow on your face, looking spiritual and fulfilled. It's natural to want these things, but they also become a trap. People go around presenting a front and denying the feelings they're really having.

If you're desperately unhappy and are really with your unhappiness, that is much more to the point than if you're beaming happily and numb inside. It is also truer practice. Mindfulness doesn't make you happy all the time. When you're experiencing fear, or abject terror—and no one *wants* to feel these things— there is a definite fulfillment when you're really with it. It isn't a sense of accomplishment, exactly. It's that you're living your life as it is right now.

That's what it means to calm the mental processes. A feeling arises—even one as powerful as fear—and, using the conscious breathing, you stay with the feeling, stay with it, stay with it. You let it be. Conscious breathing and mindfulness take the power out of the feeling so it doesn't condition the mind to get hysterical. Our feelings lose their potency to propel us into these unwise states.

That is what the Buddha finally said about feeling. "The enlightened one has become liberated and freed from all attachments by seeing as they really are the arising and passing away of feelings. The relishing of them, the danger from them, the release of them."

NO ESCAPE

These four contemplations of the second tetrad have concerned themselves with our need to know our feelings, which are a whole world; they're going on day and night. The practice is really to get to know them, to see what brings them about and how they pass away. Also to see—especially in the seventh and eighth contemplations—how they condition the mind.

The Buddha's teaching begins with the fact that there is suffering in the world. That was what attracted me to the practice in the first place, that it begins by admitting we're all ignorant and suffering. He's not saying suffering is all there is, but that there definitely is suffering. There is also an end to suffering, which comes about through the seeing of it. We can't neglect that step. We need to take a long hard look at our suffering.

The practice really begins when you see that there is no escape from suffering—not that there isn't an end to suffering, but that escaping is not the means to that end. We started with the breath and the body, fairly simple processes, then moved on to the feelings, which for most people are more complex, highly charged. There is a greater possibility for suffering in them, also perhaps a greater potential for happiness.

It isn't, as people mistakenly think, that we shouldn't have feelings. It isn't even that we shouldn't prefer to feel something that is pleasant, or run from something that is unpleasant. The problem is that we're enslaved to these tendencies; we expend endless energy running after and away from things. Just look at our society as a whole, with its absolutely ceaseless and manic quest for pleasure. Desire isn't necessarily a bad thing, but we need to see how pervasive and driven this whole tendency is, and bring some balance to it, so that we give ourselves some choices.

When we're not aware of our feelings, we're driven by them, pushed around. There's a frenzied quality to our day; we react automatically, without really noticing our feelings. The practice is just *to* notice them, to experience them thoroughly and fully. That is what the Buddha called wise attention. It gives you freedom to respond to things or not. Every little thing doesn't knock you for a loop. You begin to see that it's all workable. You develop some equanimity.

Finally, as we'll see later on in the sutra, you learn the true nature of feelings, that they arise and pass away and are empty of self. That doesn't make you appreciate them less. Actually, once you're not enslaved to them, you can appreciate them more. You move to a place of deeper fulfillment, what in Dharma circles is sometimes called your true nature, or Buddha nature.

But the way to freedom in the world of feelings is to go into them; you can't go over or around them. It's the same thing we were saying earlier about rapture and peace. Both of these states have great attractions and advantages, and both have obvious pitfalls; if you get attached to them, you create suffering, and you also don't work on your negative feelings.

But what we said about these powerful states—and it may be a little clearer now—is that you can come to know them thoroughly. You can see what use they are (especially peace, which can be a great source of renewal) without being enslaved to them. Being free doesn't mean you don't feel them. You just approach them differently.

And if you can handle powerful feelings like these, lesser feelings are child's play. You can find the same kind of freedom in your whole life.

PUSHING YOUR BOULDER

I'd like to end our discussion of feelings with an unusual example, the myth of Sisyphus, which people don't usually connect with Buddhism, but which the Zen teacher Charlotte Joko Beck has used in her teachings. It has been extremely helpful to me; and actually, if Buddhist principles have any real truth, they should apply to any tradition. Experts on Greek myth may quarrel with my interpretation. I'm obviously using the story for my own purposes.

I come in at the end: Sisyphus has done something to displease the gods, and for his punishment he is condemned to push a boulder up a hill for eternity. No sooner does he get it to the top than it rolls back down, and he has to push it up again. When I heard this story as a college student, it was absolutely terrifying to me, nothing to do with pushing a rock, of course, but the fact that the punishment went on for eternity.

Now I look at this story and it seems to be about all of us. Think of what we said earlier about the endlessly repeating tasks that make up our day. Think of the example that I gave from Thailand, when we were sweeping the path clear of leaves even as they were falling on the part we had already finished. Think of anyone, anywhere, who does housework.

This story seems to describe the texture of our lives. But it is usually interpreted as a definition of hell.

One aspect of the difficulty is the tremendous repeating disappointment that Sisyphus faces. He's pushing the boulder to get it to the top of the hill. And when he gets it there—it's usually portrayed as a tremendous struggle—he'd probably like to feel some sense of accomplishment, if not actually receive a reward. That never happens. There isn't even a momentary pause in which to enjoy the accomplishment. The rock just rolls back down.

You can imagine the tremendous suffering the mind could create out of that. It is the mind, actually, that would make it into hell. You may also see a similarity with practice. We begin with a hope of some reward—if not enlightenment, which does seem fairly remote, at least a feeling of relaxation. But as long as we sit looking for that, we're not going to find it. We also won't really be doing the practice. Practice doesn't begin until we see that there is no escape from this simple activity, watching this in-breath, this out-breath. Even if we achieved the thing we're calling enlightenment, would it be any different? I don't see how. We'd still have to watch our life in the next breath moment.

Suppose we are sentenced for the rest of our lives, or for all of eternity, to push a boulder up a hill. From the point of view of practice, your strategy would be to look at that fact clearly, and at all the feelings that come up around it. A major part of our suffering would be the feelings we have around it, that we should be doing something different, something with more variety, something of benefit to mankind. (Do these complaints sound familiar?) But maybe at some point we would see that this is just the way it is. There is no escape. The rest of eternity is just pushing that rock.

What I would suggest in that situation is that we just be with the experience of pushing, moment after moment, pushing that boulder up that hill. Don't get caught up in thoughts about it, just do the pushing, be the pushing. Drop any need for reward, for acknowledgment. Do we ever really get that, in any way that's meaningful? And in any case, we're then in the next moment, with more pushing, or more something.

The practice is to get into this extremely intimate fine-grained link with the present moment. Pushing the boulder. Pushing the boulder. I have found it to be an amazing experience. Instead of creating elaborate scenarios for what you should be doing, you just push the boulder. Do the dishes. Fill out your income tax. Follow the breathing.

Many of the problems that people have with the practice—and with their lives—come out of similar situations. I've heard countless people talk about it—I've also had the experience myself—so I feel as if I've got some credentials here. Most of the time that people get discouraged with practice, they do it to themselves. They've heard time and time again that the practice is being nobody and going nowhere, then they sit down and try to be somebody getting somewhere. Thoughts arise around that wish, and they suffer.

The only way out of that suffering is to take life breath by breath. Not to say, "I've been at this crummy job thirty years; how come I never get anywhere?" but to come to each moment in a fresh way, with what Suzuki Roshi called beginner's mind. Look at each breath as if for the first time. In real practice, you're dying and being born from moment to moment. Everything is new.

Many of us are attached to the past, often because of pain that we've suffered. I have worked with a number of Vietnam veterans, for example, men who have been unable to let go of their memories of the war. That might be out of a sense of guilt, or some feeling of how much of their lives they gave to it. I've also known a number of people who were in Nazi concentration camps and who were still living through their experiences fifty years later, unable to let go of them. The most vivid—and bitter—fact in their lives was the memory of that camp.

The practice does not in any way trivialize or belittle such experiences. They most definitely have to be lived through, fully experienced and mourned. All of us have difficult experiences in our past. But we have to move through them and arrive in the present moment. Life is a precious gift, it's all we have, and it is always happening in the present.

Maybe you're not the theoretical beginner to the practice whom I've been addressing all along. Maybe you've been at it for years, you have a daily practice of so many hours, you've been on all kinds of retreats, read any number of books; last week you had a really great sitting, you had three or four of them in fact; so you sit down today and it's supposed to be like *this*. But it's like *that*. Maybe you think that if you could only calm down you could really practice, or if you could just stop having sexual fantasies, or get rid of your fear. The practice, finally, is to open up to all that, to let it be, let life be what it is. To push your boulder.

Awakening isn't on the other side of those things. It isn't the day you finally push the boulder up the hill and it stays. (*Then* what would you do?) It's right there in the midst of the pushing. It has to do with letting go of that which brings torment and suffering to whatever we do.

Finally the problem is the "I." *I* pushed this boulder up this hill, *I* finally got it here, and look what happened. Awakening is dropping the "I" and just doing the pushing. Whatever your particular boulder is, bring that attitude to it and see what happens. If the practice doesn't help you there, in the greatest diffi-culty—or the most banal fact—of your life, what use is it? The practice is for the whole of your life, not some part that is sec-tioned off and called spiritual. It is available for every moment.

3

Breathing with the Mind

SITTING LIKE A FROG

We have been exploring worlds in the first eight contemplations, worlds we didn't know existed or that we took for granted.
There is the whole fascinating world of the breathing, for instance. Thich Nhat Hanh says he has been watching the breath
for fifty years and it only grows in interest. There is the vast
world of the body, which can be extremely rewarding to explore,
especially for those of us who have realized—perhaps only as
we've begun to practice—that we have been alienated from it for
years.

There is the attractive world of specific feelings like rapture
and peace, which can be almost too seductive. And there is the
whole world of feelings in general, which as we come to know
them seem not so alien, so menacing, as they once did. We get
intimate with our feelings. We're no longer tyrannized by them.

With the third set of contemplations, we stand at the threshold
of another vast world, one still more complex, that of the mind.
In Pali the word is *citta*, and it means more than mind as we think
of it, something more like mind/heart. It is much larger than the
thinking mind but includes it. If the whole *Anapanasati Sutra* is
about self-knowledge, we have arrived at a rich source of it.

It is where we have been headed all along. Everything comes

from mind, Buddhism famously says, and mind is definitely where many of our problems originate. What we have been doing with the first eight contemplations—including the important eighth one, calming mental processes—is getting to a place where we can study the mind, where we're ready to undertake the ninth contemplation.

These early contemplations—though also a rich source of knowledge—have contributed a certain calm that is necessary to move effectively into the mind itself. If the mind lacks stillness, it is difficult to examine. Anyone who has practiced meditation even a little knows how captivating and overwhelming thoughts can be. The first eight contemplations help us develop this calm. The mind becomes more and more like a clear mirror.

To some extent, in our culture, we associate calm with a certain relaxed dullness, like lying in a hammock on a summer afternoon after a hard day's work. On the other hand, we are often alert but tense, as when we face danger or financial problems. We go back and forth between these two states, relaxed but dull, alert but tense. We associate alertness with a crisis mode.

But this polarization is not intrinsic to human consciousness. What we're gradually learning in this practice is utter calm that is also highly alert, like the frog that Suzuki Roshi used to talk about, sitting on a lily pad. The frog looks entirely at its ease, rather like a small Buddha. But when a fly comes by— unfortunately for the fly—the frog proves to have been alert all along.

Different people find different aspects of the practice challenging, but for most people we have been moving in a direction of greater subtlety, and with the ninth contemplation we open up to a whole new level.

> 9. One trains oneself: "Sensitive to the mind, I breathe in. Sensitive to the mind, I breathe out."

A Buddhist master named Tang Hoi added a footnote to this contemplation. He had the unique distinction of bringing both anapanasati—this teaching from Theravada Buddhism—and Zen to Vietnam. Thich Nhat Hanh traces his lineage through this man. Tang Hoi had a way of alluding to this whole preparation for examining the mind that is vivid and inspiring. He speaks of *realizing* the breathing practice, which means seeing the breath vividly, making attention to the breath continuous.

"When the yogi has realized the breathing process," he says, "the mind is ablaze with light. Using that light to observe deeply, nothing can enter the yogi's mind that he does not see."

It is as if the murky shadowy place that we call the mind—where so much happens that we don't understand—is suddenly bright and clear, like a large empty room. According to Tang Hoi, it is attention to the breath that brings that transformation about.

Of course, there is no way you could have gone through the first eight contemplations and not seen a great deal about the mind. Especially in contemplating feelings, when we spoke of our reactions to them—pleasant, unpleasant, or neutral—we were dealing with aspects of mind. As far back as the first two contemplations—whether the breath was long or short—we were using the mind, and when you just follow the breathing, the first instruction, what you are likely to see around it (whether you want to or not) is the mind in all its confusion. The thought of examining that confused place is a daunting one. But now we're talking about a mind that we *can* look at, because it has achieved a certain calm. It is also more at home with a wide variety of mind states.

POISONS OF THE MIND

The Buddha emphasizes over and over that we are enslaved to the mind. By being attached to its contents, we are propelled into actions that cause suffering for ourselves and others. The purpose of his teaching is to free us from this attachment, to master the mind. But you don't accomplish that task by brute force. It is clear seeing that makes us true guardians of the heart.

There are three aspects of the mind that are extremely important to understand, what are called in Pali the *kilesas*, translated into English as defilements, or poisons. They are greed, hatred, and delusion. There are other aspects to this contemplation, but getting to know these states is at its heart. Equally important is knowing the mind when it is free of them.

The first one, greed, is sometimes rendered as wanting or craving or lust—not lust in its modern, sexual sense, but lust for anything. It can be for a person, but it can also be for food, drink, money, material possessions, fame, power. It can be a wish for a particular outcome in the political world. It can even be a wish for some spiritual attainment, to master anapanasati, to attain enlightenment.

It is a quality of reaching out, grasping, holding on to. It is a perfectly natural human function, which probably enables us to get food and put a roof over our head and propagate the race. It also, of course, leads to all kinds of crime, even war.

Let me give a simple example. In the interviews I do, I often encourage students to enter into a meditative dialogue with me, and at a recent one I said, "What is in the mind right now?" The woman I was sitting with had a clear mind at that moment, calm and peaceful, but then—very mildly, but clearly discernable—the thought came to her, "I don't want this to end." However natural and harmless that might seem, it was an example of wanting. She saw in the midst of her calm that little bit of perturbation, or suffering. Because she saw it, it went away. I asked her how the mind was then. "Very nice," she said, "with that wanting gone."

That's the first question with any of the kilesas: is it present? A major part of the challenge is just seeing it. As you see different kinds of craving, you'll notice that some are easy for you to deal with, some quite difficult. It is also sometimes shocking to see what the mind is taken up with, the way it spends its day, perhaps in sharp contrast to what you're actually doing, or to your sense of who you are.

This contemplation is about thoroughly experiencing the mind, moment by moment. It isn't the kind of self-knowledge that you acquire in a workshop or on a retreat or by reading a book (even this book) or doing therapy. You don't acquire it at all. It is an ongoing activity, a lifetime endeavor, not a finite process in which fulfillment comes at the end. Fulfillment comes in the doing. It can be wonderful to see something about ourselves, even when what we're seeing is not especially wonderful.

My interview with that woman was a good example: there was calm; a wish to perpetuate the calm, which disturbed it; a seeing of that wish; the passing away of the wish. It was the seeing that made it disappear. A certain amount of what we're doing is a kind of reeducation, a clear seeing of what has been happening all along. You are the teacher and the taught. You can read books like this one, listen to tapes, go to talks: all those things aim you in the right direction. But finally, you're not studying Buddhism. You're studying you. If you know all about Buddhism but don't know about you, you've missed the whole point. As Suzuki Roshi said, "When you are you, Zen is Zen."

This principle was brought home to me some years ago when I taught a ten-week introduction to vipassana meditation. The group included two Ph.D.s with a special interest in Buddhism and an intense Marxist from Yugoslavia with a Ph.D. in political science. All three were working at Harvard. The Marxist made his attitude toward religion clear: it was a subject for idiots. He was learning meditation because his girlfriend had raved about it and he was afraid he'd lose her if he didn't show some interest. The Buddhists, on the other hand, were quite reverent.

At the end of the ten weeks, the Marxist had done beautifully, growing inwardly a great deal because he had followed the instructions and practiced every day. The Buddhist scholars, on the other hand, had gotten nowhere. They had tremendous interest in the Buddha's mind but very little in their own. The whole point of meditation was lost on them.

Let's imagine that you do take an interest in your mind, and that in a given moment the mind is craving. You don't condemn it; you just see it. Perhaps, as the woman at the interview did—but don't let me persuade you; see for yourself—you see that there's suffering to that. Maybe in the seeing the craving disappears and—if only for a moment—you're just with the breathing. You see how pleasant it is to live in a mind without the craving.

That simple seeing—in the most naive way imaginable, as if for the first time—is a kind of organic intelligence. We suffer when we crave. Such learning can revolutionize the way we live. But just hearing about it is not enough. You have to see it for yourself. You have to do firsthand, personal research.

The second kilesa is hatred, or aversion, and in a sense it is the opposite of the first. Greed is a reaching out, a holding on to, while hatred is a striking out against, pulling away from, trying to avoid, any situation where we're averse to what is happening. We want to rid ourselves of it, to annihilate what offends us. Greed is when we want something that isn't there. Aversion is when we don't want something that is.

The most obvious example of this state is anger. Again, to practice, we're not at war with it. We don't try to do anything about it. If we did, that would just be more aversion. We just see what the mind is like with anger in it. We approach it with respect and take real care of it, thoroughly experience it.

The third kilesa is delusion, or confusion, and is a little harder to pin down. One example is when the mind is dark: it's as if there's a shadow cast over it, and we don't see clearly. We're confused, ambivalent, indecisive. It's a kind of running around in circles, a self-doubt. We don't know if we are wise or foolish, if we should observe or just act out.

When we're craving, we tend to overestimate the attractiveness of objects in the mind. We want something and think it would be absolutely marvelous. When we're aversive, we underestimate them. We dislike someone and think he's the most contemptible worm on earth. When we get to delusion, it's more as if we don't know what's what; life is not in focus. We don't know what's good or bad, whether to go forward or back, whether to go meditate or sit down and read (maybe a book on Buddhism!).

Delusion—or ignorance—is the primary kilesa; it is out of ignorance that the others are born. Because we can't see clearly, we spend a great deal of time running after things that don't make us happy, striking out at what is unpleasant, running away from things that can't really harm us.

There is nothing exotic about these states. We're familiar with all of them. The question is, can we practice with them? Can we see them without judging, without trying to change them, and especially without acting on them? Usually when we feel craving, we just want to take action. Eat the brownie, win the prize, whatever. If we feel aversive, we want to get out of there, annihilate the situation in some way.

Confusion may be the most difficult of all. There is a great value placed on decisiveness in our world, being strong, bold, knowing what to do. So when we're confused, we want to choose one thing or another, get away from the discomfort. The challenge for the practice is to stay with it, see what the energy of confusion is really like. Clear and deep seeing into confusion is the most reliable road to genuine clarity and decisiveness.

I had an interesting encounter with this kilesa many years ago when I was a college professor. Every year many of the seniors would come to me in the fall and say they didn't know what they were going to do the next year. Get a job, go to graduate school, go to professional school, travel for a while: all the usual choices. Their parents were very much involved, and full of anxiety. It was a highly charged situation.

I was starting meditation practice and would use a little of what I was learning with my students, just saying, "Look. You're confused, and it's all right." The tendency was to impose some false clarity. I would encourage them to let the confusion be there, because that was the truth of the moment, not to see it as some major failure (you're twenty-one and don't know what you want to do with your life!) but as a mental state that would come and go like any other.

By the end of the year, 90 percent of the students had made a decision. They would come to me and announce it with absolute finality: dentistry, or the law, or social work. It was often terribly unconvincing: they hadn't been able to stand the anxiety and had just taken a stab at something. I always admired the few students who were able to acknowledge their confusion openly, who ended the school year without having decided.

When you're feeling confusion, don't see it as interfering with your practice. It *is* your practice; it is your life in that moment. Stay with it and thoroughly examine it. Allow confusion to take you to clarity. The decision that finally emerges is likely to be much more dependable. It isn't the frightened ego reacting to a situation that feels uncomfortable. It is a natural process that is gradually unfolding.

Kyudo Roshi says it beautifully in Lawrence Shainberg's *Ambivalent Zen*, advising his student in a moment of doubt: "Can't decide? Ah, great decision, Larry-san! My teacher, he say, 'If you confused, do confused. Do not be confused by confusion.' Understand? Be *totally confused*, Larry-san, then I guarantee: no problem at all."

EXPERIENCING THE MIND

The challenge of the ninth contemplation is to experience the mind thoroughly and fully just as it is, with whatever level of clarity we have. As we do that, we begin to see that mindfulness takes the energy out of our mind states, so that they arise but no longer have so much power to push us around. We no longer act automatically at their commands.

There is then not as much suffering if a difficult emotion comes up, even something as strong as anger or fear. We've grown intimate with these mind states, and that changes our relation to them. They are coming from our own storehouse of consciousness, right out of our hearts. We are learning to observe these states in a friendly way, instead of identifying with them, resisting them, or rejecting them.

The point is to change our mind from a battlefield, where we're always fighting these states, or getting lost in them, to a place of peaceful coexistence. Then these visitors, these guests in consciousness, don't have such power.

What we will eventually see, when we come to the thirteenth contemplation, is that they are all impermanent and lack a substantial self. Right now we're mainly learning to recognize and open up to them, but we can't help sometimes noticing that they arise and pass away.

It's like the mosquito bite that we talked about earlier: anger, when you look at it closely, is not a steady stream of emotion but a complex state that is constantly changing in intensity and finally disappears altogether. Anger is a movement of energy that comes and goes. It can't possibly characterize a human being. It doesn't have any enduring substance.

As we see everything coming and going—the breathing, feelings, mind states—we begin also to see that the whole notion of a *self* who is *doing* these things is imaginary. As that lifelong notion falls away altogether—or at least weakens—we drop a heavy burden. We can rejoice in our self-knowledge; it's not a grim assignment that we're condemned to carry out all the time but a helpful practice that is making our life lighter. We tap into a certain joy at the heart of the practice.

In time—as you see them again and again—these mind states lose their potency. It is not necessarily a problem to be visited by anger or craving or fear. This isn't an ideology—"It's okay to be fearful"—but an actual fact: you're fearful, and it's all right. It becomes easier to turn to these states and experience them directly, just as it has become easier to allow each breath to follow its own nature.

When that happens, these states start thinning out, falling away. The direction of meditation is for everything to go back where it came from. It comes out of stillness and goes back to stillness. As the mind grows quiet and still, our sense of psychological time falls away and we open up to a vast spaciousness. It has been there all along, behind our agitation.

The ancients spoke of the sky that is beyond the clouds. The productions of the mind are like clouds, some beautiful, some dark and threatening, but they are all clouds in the sky of the mind. The sky is vast, glorious, and unchanging, was never born and never dies.

Most of us live at the level of the clouds. We barely know there is a sky. And the way to the sky is through the clouds, by studying them, observing them carefully in a friendly and unbiased way. In time, as we do that, they pass away, the same way a feeling passes away when we bring mindfulness to it. Then we open up to something altogether different, vast and silent, full of energy and love, of every kind of nourishment we need. We realize it has been there all along.

EPIC OF THE HEART

We can also look at the kilesas from another angle, try to characterize what is happening in a slightly different way. Let's say that the job of practice is to guard the citta, the mind/heart, because it is the most valuable possession we have. In a way it is all we have. It is what we are. *Anapanasati*—or mindfulness itself—is sometimes called the guardian of the heart.

What we've got here is an epic drama, the most important battle imaginable. On one side the kilesas, greed, hatred, and delusion. On the other side—standing alone—are mindfulness and wisdom. The word for these qualities in Pali is *satipanna*. *Sati* is mindfulness. *Panna* is discernment, a clear seeing. *Satipanna* is mindfulness accompanied by discernment, a direct precise seeing in the moment.

For most of us, the kilesas are far stronger than our wisdom. Much of our life is spent in greed, hatred, and delusion, one grand scheme after another. We don't think we're acting out of those states, of course; we think we're working in our best behalf. We think the things we want are beneficial. We feel that way because of ignorance, which is powerful and all-pervading.

Awakening, finally, is seeing through ignorance.

But as we start off, the heart is smothered and exhausted by years of these mind states. We all show up with a slightly different package. One person is frequently greedy; another is angry; another is often confused. We have put in a certain amount of time out in the world, and we have seen that our unexamined impulses propel us into unfulfilling actions. Out of those who see that, a much smaller group wants to do something about it. They begin Dharma practice.

They find, typically, that the kilesas are strong. Wisdom is weak.

That's one of the reasons we need the whole structure of practice—teachers and centers and retreats and sanghas—because, especially at first, wisdom needs help. Actually, however, all the wisdom we need is inside us, where this epic drama is taking place. Our worst enemy is not outside of ourselves. Our worst enemy is in our own heart. Our best friend is there too.

One of the most radical aspects of the reeducation that this practice involves is not to locate our problems outside ourselves but always to look inside. The kilesas are brilliant at making us look outside; they keep us constantly occupied, so we never look into our hearts.

We don't just make that mistake on a personal level. Our whole society does it. We spend all kinds of time and money going after drug traffickers, whom we locate south of some border. We try to intercept and annihilate them. We never ask why we have such a need for drugs in the first place, without which they would be powerless.

My favorite example of that tendency—on a lighter note—comes from my grandfather. He had come to this country from rural Russia, where he never even owned a necktie, but here, on special occasions, he sometimes had to wear one. He hated that, because he had so much trouble tying it properly. One end always came out too long.

There was always considerable agitation around the house as he tried to perform this intricate task, usually while everyone was waiting, and finally—after a number of unsuccessful attempts—he would spit and pronounce a curse in Yiddish. "The cholera should afflict Christopher Columbus!" The man had impeccable (if rather elaborate) logic. He was blaming his failure to knot a tie on the European who had discovered the country where he now had to wear one.

We want to look everywhere but inside ourselves for our problems. As long as we do that, we will never get to the root of them. Several years ago, my practice took a real turn when a certain conclusion became overwhelmingly clear: there is no escape from suffering. Realizing that fact gave me a whole new energy for practice, a kind I'd never had before.

That is what the Buddha is saying. There's an obvious fact about our lives, sitting right in front of us, and we've been ignoring it. That's what ignore-ance is. The practice, instead, is to make it our highest priority to be with our experience, just as it is, right now.

The difficult thing about practice isn't learning to sit for an hour, or sit for a weekend, or go on a three-month retreat, as hard as those things are. The difficult thing is to pay attention to what is happening right here and now. It is the kilesas that keep us from doing that. And the way to break their spell is to turn and look directly at them, to see these mind states just as they are. That is the way out of ignorance and toward freedom.

METHODS OF ATTACK

This epic drama I've been talking about, this grand battle between ignorance and wisdom, is characterized differently in different traditions. In the Thai forest tradition teachings of Ajahn Maha Boowa, the kilesas are the enemy. They are brilliant and powerful. They permeate the heart. They are so intelligent that they can disguise themselves as friends, so subtle that we sometimes can't even see them. This is a war. We should take no prisoners.

One time Ajahn Maha Boowa was chiding a monk right beside me, really lacing into him. The monk had absentmindedly put his cup near the edge of a table where it could have been knocked off and broken. I don't speak Thai, so everything had to be translated for me. Ajahn Maha Boowa looked around and saw my translator and said, "Tell him I'm not attacking the person, only the kilesas." He wanted to make sure that I knew the difference.

When I first heard that rhetoric, I wasn't terribly drawn to it. *This* is Buddhism? There's so much aggression in it. But the tradition goes back to ancient texts, and is saying, "Watch your step. Your life is at stake here, and the lives of people you care for. Pay attention!" It's trying to convey the urgency of practice, to remind us what we are up against.

Thich Nhat Hanh represents another tradition. His strategy, in effect, is to emphasize love of the kilesas, the same way Jesus said to love our enemies. That keeps you from creating a situation that is angst ridden and dramatic, and from setting up a dualism full of conflict and struggle. You don't see the kilesas as alien foreign bodies but as parts of yourself, to be accepted with love. Thich Nhat Hanh also represents an ancient tradition, which he has consciously adopted to work with Westerners, many of whom tend to be dualistic and aggressive anyway.

There is truth in both of these approaches. More and more as I teach and practice, I see that the kilesas really are powerful and dangerous forces, and, if anything, practitioners take them too lightly. These forces can do a great deal of harm. But it is also true that attacking them, wishing they didn't come up, does not work; they have to be accepted as parts of consciousness and allowed to flower so that you can see just what they are, really come to know them, and allow them to disappear. We don't want to take too soft an attitude, because that doesn't show a proper respect for the power of these states. But we also don't want to attack them.

Both of these approaches are essentially metaphors. They both have advantages and problems, because no use of language can cover everything. Ajahn Maha Boowa is not trying to nourish aversion; Thich Nhat Hanh is not promoting unawareness. The practice is finally not about what words we use to characterize the kilesas; it is about direct attention to them, clear seeing of them. That is what frees us.

PICK UP YOUR LUNCH BUCKET

It is helpful to remind ourselves, especially as we get further along in the sutra and the teaching gets more complex, that what we are discussing is blue-collar work. You can talk about it all you want, but what it comes down to is observing your mind in this moment, just as it is, even now, as you are reading. You never escape from this task. When you think you have, that you're in a situation where you don't need to watch the mind, that is just one more idea in the mind: thinking you've escaped.

People try so many things to find fulfillment, even spiritual fulfillment; they run around exhausting themselves. The Buddha's teaching is that everything is right where you are, right now: your suffering, and the end to your suffering. There's no reason to go anywhere. What you need to do is look into your mind, which is itself a space, in fact an infinite space. It is colored by the energy that is coursing through it in the moment, often one of the three possibilities we've been talking about: greed, hatred, and delusion.

The Buddha told a story to illustrate the way we often confuse desire—and the satisfaction of desire—with happiness. There was a leper who lived in the forest and suffered from terrible pain and itching. The only way he could relieve himself was to dig a huge hole, fill it with burning wood—thereby creating hot charcoal—

and rub his afflicted body against the charcoal. He could only get relief by creating another kind of suffering.

The story goes that he was cured and moved to the city to lead a normal life. Sometime later he had occasion to return to the forest, and there he saw lepers relieving themselves as he had once done, rubbing themselves against hot charcoal. He couldn't watch. It was just too painful.

That is what the Buddha says our lives are like. In order to relieve ourselves from one suffering—our yearning—we create another, with all the things we run after to relieve it. A healthy person, who has gotten over the illness we suffer from, finds it painful to watch us, putting ourselves through all this suffering in the hope of relieving suffering.

If this doesn't sound right to you—if it doesn't seem that desire is suffering—then there's no problem. Just go around desiring things and trying to satisfy yourself the way everyone else does. Our culture is built around that activity. We have the greatest consumer culture in the world. We create more and more things to do, better this and better that. We don't, however, seem to get happier and happier.

Perhaps someday we'll see that acquisition doesn't lead to happiness. Just as my practice really began when I realized I couldn't escape my sorrow, someone else's will begin when it becomes apparent once and for all that desire is suffering. The person will look into his or her mind and see craving, and simultaneously see that suffering is inevitably a part of it.

That is the first step, just seeing it. Then you have to be with it, really meet it, eye to eye. You have to stay with it for as long as it's there, this yearning that is a form of suffering. And then you see it pass away. So you know what it's like to have that yearning. You know the whole experience from beginning to end. When you've done that enough times, you're not worried about it anymore. It's just that same old yearning.

That doesn't mean you give up all the potential objects of craving: food, sex, money, power, fame. It means that you're not enslaved to them. You can take them or leave them, even something like fame. Fame itself is not suffering. It is just the fact that a lot of people know who you are. But it is a rare person, it seems, who can handle fame. It becomes the object of all kinds of yearning and grasping and attachment.

It is also important to see what the mind is like when yearning is not present, when you're not experiencing that form of suffering. You might arrive at a moment when the mind is clear, and you can follow the stillness and breathing and take a certain joy in that, just because the suffering of desire is not there. You begin to see that there is no peace or joy in desire, but a great deal in its absence. That can be an important fact to realize. The mind naturally starts to incline itself toward clarity and inner silence. It doesn't need exhortation in Dharma talks. It enjoys and values contentment.

The same thing is true of aversion. Anger is a good example. Not only does it lead to suffering—it can lead to a lifetime in prison if it goes far enough—but anger itself is suffering. It's a fire that rages in the mind. Usually we are much more interested in who started the fire than in putting it out; we go on and on about the object of our anger, and meanwhile we're burning up. What's the difference who started it, if there's nothing left of you?

The challenge of this practice is just to turn to the fire. Examine what it is to be on fire, to be raging with anger. Approach it with a mind of innocence, a naïveté. Open up to it and stand within it. Drop all your ideas and theories and just stay with it. Don't try to put it out. See what anger is without the concept, without even the word *anger*; just see the energy. Let the fire rage, meet it consciously, so that you can learn about its cost to you firsthand.

There is also the other side of that mind state, when there is no anger in the mind, not even mild kinds like whining and complaining. Maybe you didn't have the best parents, or the best brothers and sisters, or go to the best schools, or have a successful first marriage. But in this moment, for whatever reason, all that doesn't bother you. You're calm and at peace. You're not feeling aversion. Seeing that is extremely important. It's the beginning of a process of reorchestrating your energy.

The last mind state is confusion. See what the mind is like when it's running around in circles, when it's ambivalent, when there is a shadow over it, a feeling of puzzlement. When the mind is dull or in conflict, when it's hesitant and without confidence. Get to know that mind and also get to know the mind when confusion is absent, when everything is clear. The sky is really blue, the grass is really green. You're hungry and you know it. Or there's a feeling that you've often taken for hunger, but you realize it's just a yearning in the mind. You then know what the mind is like when it's clear, which is an important part of the path.

The challenge of the ninth contemplation is to know the mind in all these states. They're not limited to sitting, of course. They're happening all the time. The practice is to be able to turn to them more and more, with the breath as a help, and see them happening: now wanting, now rage, now confusion, now their absence, all accompanied by mindfulness and the conscious breathing. You're not trying to make these mind states happen or not happen. They happen by themselves, and you just watch.

Take attachment, for instance, mentioned over and over in the Buddha's teaching. He said that his whole teaching could be summed up by this phrase: Under no circumstances attach to anything. But attachment is a perfectly natural event. We get attached to people, notions, physical possessions.

So we learn to recognize and watch attachment, we get good at seeing when it comes up, and in time it's less of a problem. It can also be a big step in the direction of dropping the attachment completely. Is it possible for us to love someone without attachment? If not, can we see the extra that is attachment and in the process weaken its hold over us? We may be able to keep it from being destructive, take some of the ache out of the suffering that so often accompanies grasping.

A lot of us have an image of how we'll be when we're advanced in this practice, utterly present, free from clinging, anger, confusion. We also have an image of how we are now, which is far from that ideal. This practice is beyond such images altogether. It sees exactly how things are when you *do* have attachments, when you're feeling anger, even when you have an image of yourself. It doesn't envision a way you should be. It just examines how you are in this moment.

BECOMING A CHICKEN

When I first went to the Thai forest to practice, I thought I was going to a quiet idyllic place. Actually, it is noisier than the busiest sections of Boston, largely because of the wild chickens. They are extremely loud and make a constant racket. They seem to be having a wonderful time.

Ajahn Buddhadasa, my teacher there, really did like Westerners, but he also enjoyed chiding us sometimes. He used to say, "Don't you feel shamed by the chickens? They don't get insomnia, headaches, or ulcers. They are free of nervous tensions and mental disorders. People take drugs by the ton while chickens are drug-free, but they sleep tight, minds at ease. Human birth gives us a right to be neurotic, but is that a blessing or a curse? Please find some Dharma method like anapanasati before it's too late. Live happily, no longer shamed by the chickens."

In some ways, the ninth contemplation is about learning to be more like a chicken. We work with it for a while, then move on, with no pretense that we've exhausted all the subtle variations of greed, hatred, and delusion.

It is also helpful to see, looking back over the contemplations, that these mind states have been part of all of them. Even back when you were focused on the body, even when you were just following the breath, a lot of the changes you noticed had to do with mind states, though we didn't mention them at the time.

At some point, when we have become a bit more familiar with mind states, when we are starting to develop confidence that whatever turns up is directly observable, we will feel ready for contemplation number ten.

> 10. One trains oneself: "Gladdening the mind, I
> breathe in. Gladdening the mind, I breathe out."

When you are really ready to do this contemplation, it is extremely joyful and pleasant. You actually learn how to make the mind happy. Many things in life gladden the mind, and you already know what some of them are: you get a compliment, do a job well, get a promotion, make some money, have a good meal, make love, see a good movie.

This tenth contemplation points to something different: can we gladden the mind with Dharma? The Buddha said that Dharma is the greatest—also the most subtle—joy. It is not separate from the joys that we've already mentioned. But in the tenth contemplation you're not getting happy through material means or sensual means. You're getting happy through the joy of practicing the Buddha's way.

I have experienced this happiness, and so have many of the people I've practiced with. I'm not talking about enlightenment. I'm just talking about a real gratitude for the good fortune of being able to bring these teachings to life.

That can be sentimental, of course; it can be mystical, ideological, or romantic. When I first thought I had a love of the Dharma, back in the sixties, it was rather different. I suppose you could say that I had a great deal of faith in the practice; such faith includes happiness. But it was not a faith that was verified by life experience. I hadn't practiced enough.

We had all kinds of romantic notions back then about how wonderful the great Asian meditation masters were. Some of us made huge changes in our lives that involved a real leap of faith. But that faith wasn't fully ours, we didn't own it, because we hadn't tasted the fruits of the Dharma. Much of the energy and excitement came from the fantasy of an incredible spiritual undertaking with a magnificent outcome. The real fruit of practice is more fulfilling than these flashy imaginings. But we hadn't much tasted that fruit.

If you continue in the practice for a while, you discover a tangible joy, which has nothing to do with faith or ideology or imagination. Meditation practice brings a happiness that is palpable. I'd like to suggest a few ways that it might come about.

WAYS TO JOY

You're not ready for the tenth contemplation until you've reached a certain point in the practice, until you can calm the body, feelings, and mind fairly easily, until—more and more often—you remember to turn to what is happening for you in the present, just as it is. You're not tyrannized by painful states of consciousness, like fear or loneliness. Perhaps they come up, with all the power they ever had, but you know that you can be with them fully as long as they are present in consciousness and can watch them pass away. They're not a problem.

There are basically two roads to this joy. One comes out of samadhi or samatha practice, the practice of concentration. A concentrated mind is a happy mind. Even people new to the practice have experienced this fact, when they have a few moments of steady focus on the breath. It isn't that anything else is happening. The concentration itself is joyful. You learn to be with the breath more continuously, and a certain joy comes out of that.

It can't be forced; it just happens when conditions are right, like a flower blooming. Part of it has to do with the fact that you've left your worries behind, but another has to do with the naturalness of a concentrated mind. It's a wonderful talent to have, when you can concentrate the mind quickly and easily.

The other road to joy in this contemplation is vipassana, wisdom itself. You see into things very clearly, and that seeing gives you a joy that transcends what you get from a concentrated mind. The classical method would be to go back through all the contemplations from the vantage point of number ten, beginning with the simple breathing in and out. For some people who are very adept, it might take just a few minutes to experience joy from the in-and-out breath. They'd go on through all the contemplations, the joy of feeling the whole body, the joy of calming the body, the joy of being confident enough to surrender to the mind states that visit us. You can also simply take a contemplation that has been especially fulfilling for you and gladden yourself with it.

The fifth contemplation opens up to rapture. The gladness we're talking about here includes another subtle dimension, a certain joy at being able to finish something, to do it effectively. You know the feeling from other aspects of your life—some art form you've mastered, or a meal you cooked particularly well, even a simple household task. It's the feeling of taking something from the beginning through the middle to the end, thoroughly applying yourself and coming through it.

It's another form of that joy when you see that what we're talking about is actually real; you've been reading that meditation leads to peace and you've been waiting and waiting for it to turn up. Finally—as you notice one day that you've dropped into peaceful happiness—there it is. You've found this thing you've wanted for so long.

Maybe in the past you didn't get too explicit about noticing that, but here, in the tenth contemplation, you do. You see that you've come through all these contemplations and can do them. It's like being a virtuoso musician who has built up a repertoire. You have nine different ways to bring joy to the mind. There's a kind of exaltation that is intrinsic to the activity itself. The ego isn't a part of that feeling, though of course it can come in. But it's like when people have been telling you for years about an exotic fruit and how wonderful it tastes. Finally you taste it and say, Yes! It *is* delicious. You don't take it on faith anymore. You've had the experience.

But let's go back to the fifth contemplation for a moment—the rapture that naturally proceeds out of calming the breath and body—because it is particularly instructive in this regard. What you're contemplating here is not that rapture but the fulfillment that comes from being able to attain rapture. It's more like the joy of learning. Our schools have largely killed off that joy; they've made learning a matter of competition, of getting a good job, but in pure learning, the kind that Socrates and Plato spoke of—and in our own time Krishnamurti—there is real joy.

So you've read about this rapture and heard about it, but now you've made it your own. It's the joy of competence, of effectiveness, of living fully and wholeheartedly. It isn't just rapture; it's the fulfillment of being able to enter into rapture. You are starting to taste the immense joy that is possible in the contemplative life.

When you're looking with mindfulness at this gladdened mind, you can't help seeing that it's impermanent. We tend quite naturally to attach to such happiness, and suffer when—inevitably—it falls away. If we can see this link and in the process release ourselves from the grip of such clinging, we taste a kind of vipassana joy, a gladdening that comes from insight.

You're seeing the rapture and the attainment of the rapture, but you're also seeing something deeper. And that is the real point, not the temporary high you've found. This practice is not about getting high or being in a good mood. It doesn't for a moment imply that good moods are permanent, that you can be happy all the time.

This gladdening of the mind, though of course impermanent, is nevertheless extremely valuable. For one thing, it can restore the love of learning that we had as children; it restored that love to me, after it had been damaged in the highly competitive and goal-oriented atmosphere of formal education.

It also gives you a new sense that the practice is working, that all these states are possible. The Buddha said that his teaching is about suffering and the end of suffering, which sounds like an ambitious project. But it begins to seem that there really are possibilities of ending suffering, that it isn't just a desperate wish. It gives a fresh feeling to your practice, makes you approach the cushion in a whole new way.

Recently I saw a documentary film on the life of the virtuoso violinist Yehudi Menuhin. I was especially moved by seeing the joy that poured out of him as he played his instrument. For a meditator, this joy can emerge from the growing ability to immerse oneself in practice, to be at home in the midst of a wide range of mental and bodily conditions, being able to enter the rapture of a concentrated mind, being just as able to sit with equanimity surrounded by the fire of the kilesas. The Buddha was said to have mastered come-what-may seeing. We are beginning to join him, to establish a foothold in the world of Dharma practice.

There is no end to learning. Even the Buddha, though free from suffering, had countless opportunities for refinement. That is yet another aspect of the joy, that it will continue to deepen for as long as we do it. One of my favorite quotations is from the Japanese artist Hokusai, from the preface to *The Hundred Views of Fuji*. His attitude toward his art is the one we might usefully take toward Dharma practice.

> From the age of six I had a mania for drawing the form of things. By the time I was fifty I had published an infinity of designs: but all I have produced before the age of seventy is not worth taking into account. At seventy-three, I have learned a little about the real structure of nature, of animals, plants, trees, birds, fishes, and insects. In consequence, when I am eighty, I shall have made still more progress; at ninety I shall penetrate the mystery of things; at a hundred I shall certainly have reached a marvelous stage; and when I am a hundred and ten, everything I do, be it but a dot or a line, will be alive. I beg those who live as long as I to see if I do not keep my word. Written at the age of seventy-five by me, once Hokusai, today Gwako Rojin, the old man mad about drawing.

FINDING REAL NOURISHMENT

The eleventh contemplation deals with a mind state that is extremely valuable for human beings but that most of us have little experience of.

11. One trains oneself: "Steadying the mind, I breathe
in. Steadying the mind, I breathe out."

This contemplation is about getting to know the mind when it
is concentrated and when it isn't. The emphasis is not so much
on the object of concentration as on the degree of concentration
itself. If you've done the practice in the classical manner, starting
with the first contemplation and moving through them one at a
time, this meditative exercise should be smooth and easy. You
will already have developed substantial concentration. If you have
just gladdened the mind in the tenth contemplation, you are in an
even stronger position, because such meditative joy dramatically
facilitates the arising of a concentrated mind.

At the beginning of our discussion of the *Anapanasati Sutra*,
we spoke of our doggy mind, the way it runs after anything that
comes up, including many things—like that plastic bone—that
have no nourishment at all. We wanted to develop something
more like lion mind, a deep steadiness, where we don't automatically run after every bone that is tossed.

The whole sutra traces a long process of taming the mind, not
by breaking it, but actually by being very gentle with it, either
bringing it back to the breath without judgment or blame, or letting it do whatever it wants and just watching it. The image that
the ancients used for this second process was of a wild bull, which
you tame by giving it a huge pasture to run around in. A part of
that process is seeing how it all works, how feelings become mind
states and how mind states proliferate.

As you've studied these things, you've gotten used to them.
You've noticed that the mind has moved from the breath and have
gently brought it back thousands of times. And even from the
earliest stages, wisdom has come in, because one of the things
you can't help noticing is that not only do you keep chasing the
same bones, but they aren't worth chasing in the first place. They
really are made of plastic. They start to become less attractive as
you notice this. You also begin to see what a lovely thing it is
simply to be concentrated on the breathing.

You begin to ask yourself: If *this* is so fulfilling and *that* so unfulfilling, why am I doing so little of this and so much of that? You begin to see that there is a kind of peace available inside you. Your confidence in the value of a concentrated mind grows, and you naturally become much more interested in developing it.

Of great help in developing a concentrated mind are the precepts (*sila* in Pali), which we haven't talked about so far. They are not simply ethical commands like the Ten Commandments; they are more like intelligent guidelines to warn us of areas where we typically create problems for ourselves. They instruct us not to kill, not to steal, not to misuse sexual energy, not to use speech incorrectly, not to use substances that cloud the mind.

Sometimes people think that practice is only about sitting; they sit morning and evening, go on retreats now and then, and figure it doesn't matter what they do the rest of the time. But if your personal life is in chaos, how are you ever going to concentrate the mind? Sitting and the precepts flow into each other. Straightening out your daily life helps you concentrate your mind. And as your mind grows stronger and more concentrated, it is in a better position to see and restrain actions that lead to trouble.

Once you develop a certain amount of concentration, you can become almost sporting with it. I practiced with monks in Thailand who could drop into deep states of concentration—the *jhanas* we talked about earlier—at will. They didn't even have to get into a special posture. It was like stepping into an elevator and pushing a button: boom, they were in the subbasement.

When you really get good with the eleventh contemplation, you can do the same thing we did with number ten: go back through all the contemplations, one by one, and look at the role of concentration in each of them. With number five, for instance—the contemplation of rapture—you would be interested not so much in the rapture itself as in the concentration that accompanies and makes it possible.

You come to know concentration very intimately, discovering its various uses—when there is pain in the body, for instance.

When attention is fixed on an unpleasant feeling, the mind doesn't have time and space to make up stories that can turn that pain into torment. The energy of concentration in isolating the pain also reduces its intensity. Concentration becomes a real friend in times of stress.

One thing you notice is that as concentration increases, the hindrances—craving, anger, restlessness, dullness, and doubt—diminish. After all, it is the hindrances that have been pulling you away from the breath all along. As you come back to the breath again and again and gradually learn to stay with it, you become more intimate with it and see what it really is. Out of that concentration—as we've pointed out before—rapture develops, and out of the rapture a deep peace.

But that peace is followed by a still deeper state, one-pointedness, in which the mind becomes completely absorbed in the breath. It's as if you disappear into it. There is tremendous joy and peace in that state; it's a kind of nourishment. The mind is extremely still. When you come out of it, you know how valuable it has been. You have much more energy. You're clearer, more loving; you're even—however strange this may seem—more intelligent. For most of us such concentration is actually hard work, the fruit of much practice. It's not the kind of thing that will happen in a weekend workshop.

What has actually happened is that the mind has gathered its energy. All the running around that it has been doing, that doggy-mind activity, is a tremendous waste of energy. When you stop chasing around, the energy you've been dissipating is at your disposal, so that you can gather it together and penetrate to the deepest truths of reality.

The state of full concentration of the mind is called *apanasamadhi*. Once you get even a small taste of it, you want to do whatever it takes to experience it. It is a way of taking care of yourself, enabling you to taste that inner joy at the heart of concentration.

That joy, obviously, is not sensual. It comes from your nonattachment to sensual objects, which are, to some extent, what have been drawing you away from that inner place. You try to follow the breathing and are drawn away by thoughts of comfort, food, sex, trips to exotic places. But when you learn to stay with the breathing, to sink deep within your consciousness, you find that there is an intrinsic happiness there that has nothing to do with sensual pleasures, and it gives your life a whole new balance.

It isn't that you don't enjoy sensual pleasures anymore. When you're no longer so attached, you enjoy them in a different way. You don't *need* them, you're not desperate for them, because you have this intrinsic inner joy.

FACING ATTACHMENT

The twelfth contemplation—the last one on the mind—follows quite naturally from the eleventh, as we have come to expect.

> 12. One trains oneself: "Liberating the mind, I
> breathe in. Liberating the mind, I breathe out."

We're right on the edge of the contemplations on wisdom—true vipassana—because, for the first time, the Buddha now asks us to focus on liberation, which is the basis of all his teaching. "Just as in the great ocean," he said, "there is but one taste—the taste of salt—so in this Doctrine and Discipline there is but one taste—the taste of freedom." In all the steps we've gone through, whether you've noticed it or not, there has always been some interest in liberating the mind, in letting go. In this contemplation—though still not quite the liberation that will appear at the end of the sutra—this letting go is featured.

One kind of liberation follows directly out of the eleventh contemplation: as the mind gets more and more concentrated, certain tendencies go into abeyance. We have spoken already of the wanting mind, which is very insistent and makes it difficult to get concentrated. There is also the angry mind, which might pick up on some slight from earlier in the day and replay it endlessly. There is the mind when it has low energy, when it is dull. There is the opposite of that, the mind when it is extremely restless, can't stop running around. There is the mind full of worry and doubt, which can't stop questioning everything: the teacher, the teaching, and—most significant—itself.

In all of these cases, the mind gets attached to these tendencies, which are extremely powerful and don't want it to get free. They want attention right now and are formidable rivals to the breathing. One kind of liberation is just learning to stay with the breath more continuously. These mind states arise, but you catch them more quickly than you did in the past and are better able to slip out from under them. That is a kind of liberation—though momentary, because in that moment of identifying with a mind state, there is clinging, which produces suffering.

A certain fulfillment comes with that ability to stay with the breathing, a peace and joy. The power of these hindrances begins to diminish. Since you're not with them as much, you're not nourishing them. Before, when you were less aware, it was as if you were practicing being greedy or angry or doubtful. You were making these tendencies stronger. When you stop practicing them, they diminish.

Another powerful factor in their diminishment is the happiness you feel just from being with the breathing. When you really get to know that, it's much easier to avoid being pulled in by the hindrances; they're no match for the quiet fulfillment of conscious breathing. But that shift in allegiances changes the habits of a lifetime and doesn't usually happen overnight. We have to see over and over again that attention to the breath brings joy; holding on to the hindrances brings suffering.

The essence of the twelfth contemplation is to feel that liberation, to see what it is like when the mind is not attached to things. Also to notice the mind when liberation is absent, when the mind is attached and clinging. You don't suddenly subscribe to a new philosophy: attachment is bad and letting go good. You just watch these two states and see for yourself how they operate. The sure way to nonattachment is by studying, observing, and understanding attachment. There is something false about trying to let go. It is often really pushing away. Our practice is to observe the holding on.

When you are really intimate with the state of attachment, there is no thinking involved. There is no wish to let go. You surrender to the feeling of being attached. Even if you perceive it as painful, you don't try to get away. You stay with the pain until you see it is unnecessary, then you instinctively let go.

If you really get intimate with attachment, what sometimes happens is that it is transformed, and you find yourself feeling free. That might last just for a few moments, but you see what it's like. It comes about because you're not trying to do anything with the feeling; you're just letting it be.

The twelfth contemplation, then, teaches the ways of attachment and letting go. You learn about them by clear seeing, watching the mind when it clings, watching when it doesn't. And little by little, as an act of sanity, the mind prefers to go in the direction of freedom and peace and joy, and to stay away from those things which supposedly lead to happiness—and have been strongly reinforced ever since childhood—but actually don't: accumulation, getting somewhere, being someone. You find a radically new way to look at your life.

There are all kinds of attachments and many ways to suffer from them. Not long ago I read an article about poverty-stricken people in Latin America, and a part of their suffering was that they didn't have many possessions. In recent years they had acquired one—the television—which enabled them to see all the others they didn't have. The person interviewed was extremely articulate in describing the suffering he felt from not having things that other people had.

In stark contrast, I have a friend who has an extremely beautiful house, full of all kinds of antiques. It's like a museum. Around the same time as I read that article, someone came to his house and accidentally broke one of his most prized pieces. He was absolutely devastated, for weeks.

So there is the suffering of the poor, through not having possessions, and the suffering of the rich, through having too many. Both of these forms of suffering are in the mind. It's the same with many things: money, sex, food. Some people suffer from having too much, others from not having enough. There is nothing inherently wrong with any of these things. The problem is that we don't know how to use them. We make them into problems with our minds.

The monastic path handles these difficult areas by minimizing them. Many monks don't touch money, are celibate, own a few simple robes, and eat just one meal per day. That changes the parameters of the situation; although suffering can still come up, there is some protection from these highly charged areas of life. We as laypeople can't really handle the problem that way and shouldn't try to. For most of us, food is a major part of our day, our love life includes sex, and we need to use money. It is important to learn how to handle these forms of energy effectively, not flee from them in fear.

Another common area of attachment is concerned with our views and opinions. This one has nearly destroyed the world, as people wage self-righteous wars over their ethnic, religious, political, or economic ideas. Even on a smaller scale—around the dinner table or in the faculty lounge—an immense amount of suffering comes out of opinions. But the problem isn't in the opinions themselves. It is in our fierce attachment to them.

When I left academic life to study with teachers and do retreats full-time, I infuriated many of my old friends and colleagues. One accused me of having betrayed the life of the mind for "Oriental nonsense" and wouldn't speak to me for five years. He paid no attention to my attempts to share the Buddha's wisdom. It was a painful time for both of us.

Another problem area—these are categories that the Buddha listed—has to do with rites and rituals. There are beautiful rituals connected with any practice, and often good reasons for them—bowing to the altar, for instance, or bowing to other meditators—but we all know people who become obsessed with the ritual and forget the spirit behind it. Then they stand in judgment of those who don't follow it to the letter.

Finally—the most serious area, the one that interpenetrates all the rest—is attachment to things as being me or mine. Anything can become a problem, even our Dharma practice, when we think of ourselves as people who can do this or believe that or own (or not own) all of this. Finally, the fundamental basis of all suffering is attachment to things as being me or mine. It is the supreme addiction.

The twelfth contemplation is extremely straightforward in dealing with that. You sit with the breathing and notice when you are attached and when you aren't. Each mental formation will liberate itself when you observe it closely and otherwise leave it alone. Letting be and letting go become synonymous.

If, in time, you can begin to tap into the intensive happiness that I've been talking about—the peace that arises when the mind grows calm—you'll find that there is tremendous depth to it. The degree to which the mind can become absorbed is quite startling. You can drop into states of extraordinary quietude, really deafening silence. At first there is some discomfort and fear, because this state seems so foreign. The ego gets frightened because there is no place for ego in it. But eventually that anxiety diminishes and you find yourself in a place that is wonderfully silent. When you come out of that place, your life seems easier.

But it is so wonderful a place that—just as we said earlier about rapture and happiness—the mind can't help becoming attached. You discovered this place when you learned not to be attached, only to become attached to the place itself. You're in a state of peace, but there's a subtle kind of suffering involved. Also, like everything else, that state changes, and you suffer when you try to hold on to it.

It is nevertheless extremely helpful to have a mind that can

RCheck Out Receipt

Aloha Community Library
503-259-0185
www.alohalibrary.org

Wednesday, January 20, 2021 3:42:11 PM

Item: 33614075789502
Title: Restorative yoga : Relax. Restore. Re-ene
rgize
Material: Paperbacks
Due: 02/10/2021

Item: 33614082062265
Title: Elantris
Material: Paperbacks
Due: 02/10/2021

Item: 33614061075163
Title: Stay fit for life : more than 60 exercise
s to restore your strength and future-proof your
 body
Material: Paperbacks
Due: 02/10/2021

Item: 33614020175955
Title: Breath by breath : the liberating practic
e of insight liberation
Material: Books
Due: 02/10/2021

Total items: 4

Today you saved $79.97 by using your library.

Hoy ahorró $79.97 utilizando su biblioteca.

Thank You!

concentrate itself at will. Sometimes the circumstances of your life are overwhelming, and it is helpful—without repressing or denying anything—simply to step away from that for a while, to a place of peace. That is a common alternation in our practice, sitting in seclusion and stepping out into the world: to enter into a state of calm, then emerge more able to deal with whatever is going on. It is a wonderful skill to have.

At this point in our study—though life doesn't move along in this tidy way, and your practice won't either—we have gotten familiar with the body. We have intimately examined our feelings. We've taken a look at the mind itself. And now, as we're not so enslaved to the ways of the body, the feelings, and the mind, as we begin to see that the hindrances, though not eliminated, are no longer overwhelming, we are ready to go even deeper, into pure vipassana, the deep seeing into the nature of the mind-body process. That is the subject of the last set of contemplations.

4

Breathing with Wisdom

The breath can take you all the way to nirvana,
you know.

—Ajahn Fuang

KEEP YOUR EYES OPEN

In the middle of a long series of talks on the *Anapanasati Sutra*—the thirty-one talks on which this book is based—I had the good fortune to travel to India, in fact to visit the Jetavana, a retreat center donated by Anathapindika and the very place where, some twenty-five hundred years ago, on the night of a full moon, the Buddha delivered the sutra. Really it is a teaching about sixteen ways that nature functions, but nature is not something outside us, so it is also sixteen lessons about being human.

The teaching begins in a naïve, innocent way, with the most basic functions possible, looking at the ways of the breath and the body, then at the nature of feelings, finally at the variety of mind states. Watching these phenomena is like observing birds or plants or any other aspect of nature. There is endless variety, and they are always changing. You may think of yourself, for instance, as a happy person or a pessimistic person or a depressive, but if you watch your mind for any length of time, you'll see that it goes through all kinds of changes and reflects the full range of human possibilities.

By the time you get to the thirteenth contemplation—and the period of time isn't important; for some people it will be months, for others years—you've had a chance to explore yourself in a systematic and thorough way. The monks who listened to the Buddha had also done that; they were highly committed practitioners and had done a good deal of work, on their ethical behavior especially, because that was emphasized in the Buddha's teaching. They were at the end of a three-month retreat and had been watching mind states come and go all that time.

Many of them would have been practicing for years; this was just one in a long series of retreats. They had probably experienced a certain amount of bliss and deep peace. They had done other contemplations, perhaps on loving kindness and compassion. They might have developed equanimity, a certain spacious quality to the mind, so that nothing could throw them off balance, because whatever arose took place in that large space.

They may have contemplated their own death—that was common in the Buddha's day—in order to weaken the fear we all have of death and at the same time give themselves a new appreciation of a life devoted to the practice. To paraphrase the Dhammapada, one day engaged in practice is more precious than a hundred years of not practicing.

It is these monks, in any case, who were listening to the sutra and would have arrived at the thirteenth contemplation, which is in some ways the most important one. It also, in some ways, contains the remaining three contemplations in this tetrad. So we will be dealing with it at great length.

> 13. One trains oneself: "Focusing on impermanence, I breathe in. Focusing on impermanence, I breathe out."

Impermanence is not exactly big news. Poets, philosophers, songwriters, artists of all kinds, have been proclaiming it as long as humans have been around. The question is: how do you practice with it? Buddhist practice isn't just philosophical reflection, though that too can be helpful. Take a photograph from high school or college and examine how you've changed. We all still feel young; we often say we feel the same. But notice how you look.

You can also look at this phenomenon on a larger scale, that of cities, states, whole civilizations. Harvard Square—one of the most vital and exciting places in Cambridge—is constantly changing. I remember vividly one occasion when I had been on a six-month retreat and then returned. There had been an old-fashioned, homey restaurant where a bunch of us had enjoyed hanging out, the kind of place where you could have a muffin and coffee, sit and read the paper, talk to friends. But when I came back from my retreat, it was no longer there. In its place was an upscale clothing store, a window full of mannequins in all kinds of enticing poses. I had a stark realization of impermanence. I kept looking at the new store, remembering the old restaurant. The place I'd had such affection for no longer existed.

Another time, on a trip to India, I went to a museum that had a collection of many magnificent fragments of Buddhist sculpture, some more than a thousand years old. The poverty and disease of the town where the museum was located were, even for India, overwhelming. I was especially touched by the obvious malnutrition and eye disease among the children.

I was told that in ancient times the town had been extremely prosperous and included a monastery with many monks, supported by laypeople. Those people had collected what was being housed in the museum. Now all that was left was this extremely poor town, riddled with disease. Once again, the concept of impermanence struck home to me.

The Thai teacher Ajahn Chah sometimes used the world of objects to teach impermanence. Once in a talk to an aging lay disciple approaching her death, he said, "You can compare [your body] to household utensils you've had for a long time—your cups, saucers, plates and so on. When you first had them they were clean and shining, but now after using them for so long, they're starting to wear out. Some are already broken, some have disappeared, and those that are left are deteriorating, they have no stable form—and it's their nature to be like that. Your body is the same way: it's been continually changing right from the day you were born, through childhood and youth, until now it's reached old age. You must accept that. The Buddha said that conditions—whether they are internal conditions or bodily conditions—are not-self; their nature is to change. Contemplate this truth until you see it clearly."

One possible reaction to seeing impermanence is an overwhelming weariness at the fact that we attach to things that are constantly changing. Often, in our unobserved lives, we don't get this lesson. We repeat the same patterns again and again. the same resolutions every New Year, the same hopeless love affair over and over, the same argument with our spouse. Sometimes, when people really see the law of impermanence, they finally understand: it is unintelligent to attach to things that are changing.

If you want to call that wisdom, fine. Wisdom in this tradition is just a clear and thorough seeing. The words aren't wisdom, but the seeing is.

The most dramatic story I know about attachment comes from India and has to do with the way the Indians capture monkeys to use as pets. They attach coconut husks to stumps, and inside the husks they put a nut, with a few other goodies around the husk as bait. The monkey is attracted, eats the bait, then reaches into the husk to get the nut. In doing so he makes a fist, with the result that he can't get his hand out of the husk. His captors come up and take hold of him.

If he would just let go of the nut, he could go free. There's no scarcity of food; he's in the jungle, and there's plenty all around. Often the monkey is quite terrified as the captors approach, but he still doesn't let go—ignorance and greed collaborate to produce suffering. If he would let go of his attachment, he would avoid the suffering. But he doesn't.

Now and then a monkey grasps the situation clearly, lets go, and escapes to freedom. What kind of monkey are you?

When I was first giving these talks, I saw a Swedish film called *The Slingshot*, about a family of socialists in Sweden who were promoting contraception and women's rights, fighting fascism. In one scene, the police come to a public gathering and start roughing people up, breaking heads. The young son of the household climbs up into the rafters, and when he sees his father get clobbered, he looks away; he just can't take it. The father notices that. When he comes back from jail, he takes his son aside. "I saw you close your eyes," he says. "Listen, son. Revolutionaries never close their eyes."

That's what I want to say to meditators. We're learning to keep our eyes open to whatever is. That young man had a natural reaction: none of us wants to see blood and violence, especially when it involves our own father. But this practice finally teaches us that everything—the worst fear, the worst disappointment—is workable if you encounter it with clear seeing.

Avoidance doesn't work anyway. It's a tremendous waste of energy. The only thing that works is gently to turn to life as it is right now, to meet things intimately and directly. A teacher's job is just to say that, again and again: practitioners don't close their eyes.

CHANGE IS IN THIS MOMENT

The Buddha locates impermanence at the center of his teaching. There are many laws of nature, but this is the one he addresses most directly. He uses it as a door into everything else, into emptiness, into a deeper understanding of the suffering that all beings go through, into a release from that suffering.

Many of the ways of learning about impermanence that we've mentioned—looking through your high school yearbook, taking a walk through the old neighborhood—are external. The Buddha insists that we see this principle from the inside, in our own bodies and minds. Instead of observing the galaxies, the heavens, natural objects, you see that you yourself are a field of energy in a constant state of flux. You see it with an inner eye. That is the eye that you want always to keep open, the part of you that has simple intimate contact with life as you find it.

This contemplation is at the heart of vipassana meditation. It is the primary meaning of insight: clearly seeing the changing nature of all formations. When I had the meeting with Ajahn Buddhadasa that I mentioned at the beginning of the book, in which he showed me the real value of this sutra, he mentioned that one way to practice with these contemplations was to go back through all the previous twelve from the vantage point of this one.

As you do that, the emphasis is slightly different. When we originally did the first two contemplations, we were just watching the breathing. Now we are watching the way it changes in particular. Even on the simple in-and-out breath, the law of impermanence is clearly evident: no two breaths are the same. You see that fact—the way you might notice the changes in your neighborhood—but the important thing is to take it into your heart.

The emphasis in practice is on exactly what is happening in this moment. Really to learn this lesson, it is vital to be present when, for instance, a breath emerges, and also when it departs. You try to observe with a blank slate, to see the formation's birth and its death. You make that observation with all the formations, mental and physical, passing through your consciousness.

That kind of learning has the potential to be much more effective than looking at buildings around the neighborhood. Rather than reflection, imagination, logic, it is a clear seeing in the moment. What you are seeing is that you *are* impermanence.

It is also important to see the continuity of this lawfulness over a period of time. As we're observing the breath in a given sitting, we notice the many changes it goes through, as well as its effects on the body. You might move into a deep samadhi, which produces a state of rapture, and no matter how dramatic and strong that is, it is constantly changing and always comes to an end.

Beyond rapture is a deep peace, a profound stillness and quiet. Even that has subtle fluctuations and gradations. Then something comes to end that mood—a sound from outside, a frightened thought within—and it too falls away.

You can practice not just with these deep and dramatic feelings but with the countless feelings that arise and pass away in the course of a day. We're propelled into action by wanting to have good feelings and avoid bad ones, and seeing how impermanent they are can have a profound effect: we don't chase after good feelings so much, or avoid bad ones.

Even richer is the study of impermanence in the mind itself, which is what you come to when you revisit the ninth contemplation. You watch the way your mind states change all day long. Your mind might well surprise you, standing in stark contrast to what your body is doing or to the image you have of yourself. This is real self-knowledge, not what people say we are, or some idealized version we might have, but a moment-by-moment knowledge of how we actually are.

We can also visit the other contemplations on mind from the vantage point of the thirteenth. We spoke of gladness of the mind, that which is brought about through the Dharma. But the practice has a strange way of being erratic. One day you sit and feel the joy of meditation as if you're a virtuoso; the next day it's as if you've never meditated before. You can't even find your nostrils.

The same thing is true of the deep concentration of the eleventh contemplation; real absorption in it will reveal that it is a constantly changing state and that it too—like everything else—disappears. In the twelfth contemplation we experience the joy of liberating the mind, seeing how wonderful it is when something departs and we're able to let it go. But the next moment—as simple observation will show you—you're attached to something again, perhaps to the pride you feel in being able to liberate the mind.

IMPERMANENCE IS SUFFERING

When you practice the thirteenth contemplation, you focus on the constant flux of things. But impermanence itself is not the whole of what the Buddha was trying to get across. It doesn't take things far enough.

The Buddha made obscure reference to another thinker who was alive at about the same time. Ajahn Buddhadasa thinks he might have been referring to Heracleitus, the pre-Socratic Greek philosopher whose surviving work is fragmentary and who made the famous statement, "You can't step twice into the same river."

Yet Heracleitus—at least inasmuch as we know, from what survived—doesn't emphasize looking into the self. He sees change in the processes of nature but doesn't emphasize it for the individual. He doesn't draw the further conclusions that the Buddha does.

In Pali the word for impermanence is *anicca*, and a word very much related to that—a key word in Buddhism—is *dukkha*. It is usually translated as suffering, but that English word doesn't quite capture the meaning. Another (somewhat awkward) translation is unsatisfactoriness, and that gets a little closer. Dukkha is the basic unsatisfactoriness that is a part of all life. It encompasses not just the most obvious forms of suffering—sickness, old age, and death—but also the fact that even in what we think of as pleasurable moments, there is a certain basic unsatisfactoriness. Something that is inconstant cannot provide us with ultimate fulfillment.

Dukkha is inextricably linked with anicca. It isn't that one comes out of the other. It is more as if they are two aspects of the same fact.

Not long ago I saw a documentary about a killer earthquake in Japan, and it occurred to me that—from a larger perspective—it was a perfectly natural occurrence, a simple restructuring of the earth, like a change that might take place in your body. From the standpoint of certain individuals, however, it was an occasion of immense suffering.

There are countless more-mundane examples. You're sitting in a crowded room listening to a talk, and your bladder fills up. That is a natural event, which takes place all the time. But it can also be extremely uncomfortable, even embarrassing.

The Buddha is saying that really to see impermanence is to see a certain basic suffering to life. It ranges all the way from tremendous pain and sorrow to the very minor unsatisfactoriness that is a part of even our happiest moments.

A lot of people, when they hear that suffering is at the heart of the Buddha's message, don't come back to the next talk. What they're avoiding is a fact of life, not a tenet of Buddhism. You have a perfectly nice house and a hurricane comes along and wipes it out. You think you have a decent marriage and your partner suddenly leaves. The Soviet Union disintegrates—what wonderful news!—and conflicts break out all over Europe. An old friend seems to change inexplicably, and the friendship dies. And so on.

When you look at it, it all sounds pretty bleak. We manage not to notice it most of the time, but when we finally do, it is quite convincing. Then the Buddha makes the astonishing statement that there is a way to end this suffering. It isn't that you won't experience pain but that the practice will do something for the mind that will make an extraordinary difference. To take only the most difficult facts, the body will get sick, grow old, and die, but the mind doesn't necessarily have to suffer.

So impermanence is a fact, suffering is a fact, sickness and death, war, natural disaster, all are facts, but the key factor is how the mind reacts. That makes the difference between pain and torment.

Tucked inside the teaching on impermanence is a third concept, in addition to anicca and dukkha, and it is probably the most difficult of the Buddha's teachings to understand. In fact, if you are new to the practice and it seems utterly perplexing, please don't be discouraged, because it has eluded many advanced practitioners as well. I'm talking about the concept of *anatta*, or not-self.

A few years ago, a prominent behavioral psychologist who famously paced from one side of the room to the other as he lectured was the object of a prank on the part of his students. All of the students on one side of the room wore bored and sleepy expressions, barely looked at him, slouched in their seats, chewed gum. The students on the other side were bright and smiling, taking notes, nodding and responding. Sure enough, before long he was talking to only one side of the room. He had proved his own theories.

I remember that story every time I bring up anatta. Students love to hear me talk about rapture or deep states of happiness. But as soon as I talk about anatta all I see are wrinkled brows and disgruntled expressions. Afterward I get all kinds of difficult questions. (If there is no self, who gets enlightened?) For a while I actually shied away from talking about it. But whether students like it or not, anatta is an essential part of the Buddha's teaching.

He is saying that there is no enduring core to the self. It has no abiding substance. That is a curious statement to make, because our whole life is lived on behalf of notions of self that are constantly in flux. It's as if we were employed by the ego (and it's a full-time job), constantly trying to build it up. It wants more money, more possessions, more fame, better sex, a bigger car, a new house—or, if we are another kind of person, better meditation sessions, deeper samadhi, a major enlightenment experience (right now).

This process—of appropriating everything as me or mine—is constantly going on and has as its whole basis the existence of a self. That, according to the Buddha, is a delusion. It is a very high-class hallucination. We all have it. In its most extreme form it is a spiritual disease. And it is at the heart of all our suffering.

When he was asked to sum up all his teaching, the Buddha replied (to paraphrase slightly): under no circumstances attach to anything as me or mine. You can go back to any of the twelve contemplations we've just been through—this is the dark side of the practice—and see that, in one way or another, we claim all of them as me or mine.

Take the body, for instance: it gains or loses weight, starts to sag here and there, sprouts some gray hairs, and we use those facts as occasions to enhance ourselves or put ourselves down. We concoct a whole mental universe out of the physical condition of the body. The same thing is true of simple feelings—low energy, a backache—and more complex mental formations like depression or joy. We identify with them and create a self out of them. This is the process we have referred to as selfing.

But all of these things are the rough equivalent of weather conditions. They come and go, and there's nothing we can do about them. If we make them into self, we're bound to be disappointed, because they're only going to change.

What this teaching tells us is that because everything that arises passes away, a certain stress, or suffering, is an inevitable part of life. We cause that suffering by trying to hold on to these changing things, by making self out of them. The things you're identifying as self are merely mind states that you're going through. They exist, but not in the way you think they do. They're not self.

We get very caught up in the content of our mind states. People in our culture in particular give the content huge amounts of attention, especially in psychotherapy and psychoanalysis. They might spend years tracing some mental formation back to its source. But that isn't the object of Buddhist practice, and taking up the thirteenth contemplation can bring about a dramatic change in one's perspective, away from the content. You see that in a certain sense content doesn't matter, because whatever it is passes away. Every mental formation is exactly equal to every other. None has an enduring core.

We tend to dismiss and even resent that perspective. In comparison with our important thoughts, the concept of impermanence seems abstract, irrelevant, and impractical.

As a skillful teacher, the Buddha allows for our attachment to the thought process. He gives us twelve full contemplations—especially the third tetrad—to have a look at them. But at some point, when we've looked and looked, we've finally had enough. We've heard the content of our mental formations so many times we're sick of them. We're ready to move past mental formations to a deeper kind of wisdom.

ENCOUNTERING DIFFICULT EMOTION

Let's take the kind of concrete example that I've been using throughout the book, the mind state we call fear. Our usual way of dealing with it is that when fear comes up, we do something else. You get up in the middle of the night and read a book or watch television. You concoct a fantasy or some other pleasant thought to take your mind away. Maybe you actually *think* about your fear, writing in a journal, analyzing why you're experiencing fear at this particular moment in the night, what past trauma might have brought it on. You might take a tranquilizer or have a drink or call a friend on the phone. Maybe—in a worst-case scenario—you spend an hour or two absolutely ravaged by fear, lost in unawareness and identification.

In all of these situations, you're not dealing with the fear. You're seeing it as a problem. It is likely, since it isn't dealt with, to become a recurring problem, to the point where you think of yourself as a fearful person. The same process happens in any identification with fear. As soon as you say, Why am *I* having this fear? you make it into me or mine.

What the practice is suggesting is that you not see fear in this way, as part of a self. You just give total attention to the movement of energy known as fear, total mindfulness, not separating yourself from it at all, also not identifying with it. That sounds risky and frightening. Often, we are afraid to face our fear. But if you get to a point where you can do that, it is actually less frightening. It's easier than the alternatives. You see that fear is composed of strong bodily sensations and disabling thoughts. One of these thoughts might be: I am much too fearful to be able to face fear. Thinking here, and in many similar cases, actively participates in defining reality, then quickly disappears. You are left with what you take to be an objective truth: I am unable to face my fear. It is observable, and therefore workable.

What I'm describing isn't magic; it is a practice, something between an art and a science. But it can definitely be learned, and it is learned in the doing. I know of no other way.

At first maybe you try and you can't do it, though there is some relief from just being there with the conscious breathing. It puts the fear in a larger context. Perhaps you keep escaping, the way you have in the past, but you see your escapes. That can be a valuable practice too, because you see that they don't work. The mind gets tired of seeing them again and again.

Finally you get to the point where you can just be with the fear. And however monstrous it has seemed up to that point (a part of that perception stems from the fact that you have been shrinking from it), you see that it is observable, and therefore workable. You can deal with it.

You realize the futility of your escapes. They don't work. They never worked. There is a far greater fulfillment in staying with the fear. You know in some deep part of you that that is the right thing to do. And you're given confidence by the fact that the fear doesn't last forever.

It might, even in this direct facing of it, last a long time. But there are changes all along, then sooner or later the energy diminishes, and finally it disappears. Really being with it through the whole process is different from our usual intellectual understanding that it will go away. It's a different kind of knowing. And it changes our whole relationship to fear.

We see that fear isn't something we own or have any control over. We've been living as if we do, as if we should be able not to feel it. But all we can do is meet it skillfully.

It may be helpful at this point to recount an incident from my own life, an encounter with fear that was both memorable and extremely instructive. First I have to give some background information. I was a child at the time of the Second World War—nine years old on the day of Pearl Harbor—and was extremely interested in the war, following the stories every day in the newspaper.

I also heard stories that weren't in the news. Long before the Holocaust became public knowledge, Jews in the United States knew that a terrible nightmare was taking place in Europe. Perhaps partly because the stories were just whispered at first, they made a great impression on me and buried themselves in my psyche.

In later years I took a tremendous interest in Nazism, reading everything about it that I could get my hands on. I was drafted into the U.S. Army at the age of twenty, and after my training I received orders to be stationed in Washington, D.C., but I was obsessed with getting to Germany and arranged to swap orders with a married soldier who had a child and wanted to remain in this country.

I was determined to find out from the German people how the Holocaust could possibly have happened, and I spoke Yiddish, which is derived from German, so I was able to communicate with them. I felt extremely well received and got to know many Germans personally. But when I brought up that one subject, they absolutely would not address it. I came back from Germany with no more real understanding of the Holocaust than when I went.

Even when I began my academic career, in the field of social psychology, I took a special interest in total institutions: prisons, the military, mental hospitals, locked wards. My master's thesis was on race relations among chronic schizophrenics in the locked ward of a mental hospital, and behind even that subject I can see my obsession with Jews in concentration camps during the Second World War.

Now my story jumps ahead. Many years later I was doing a six-month self-retreat during the winter at the Insight Meditation Society (IMS) in Barre, Massachusetts. I had been there for three or four months, so my mind was extremely quiet, and perhaps unusually vulnerable. One afternoon I was meditating in my room, and some other meditators came into the dorm, stomping their boots to get the snow off. Suddenly—and I don't know how to describe this except as an extremely vivid set of images—I was in Nazi Germany, and those stomping boots were the SS troops coming to get me.

I felt a kind of terror that I had never experienced before, and haven't since. The horrifying visual images that kept coming to mind seemed utterly real. I was trembling, nauseous, sweating, weeping, going through deep physical as well as emotional pain. It was an extremely complicated and convincing mind state.

I had been practicing at that point for a number of years and had developed a fair amount of samadhi. In a way, I don't think that depth of fear would have come up if I hadn't been ready for it. A tiny corner of my mind knew that I was actually in Barre and that everything was all right. But most of me was in extreme pain and believed I was in great danger.

I tried to bring full attention to the images and to my physical and emotional pain. For a while I'd be mindful, then I'd slip and get caught up in things, then I'd use the breath to bring me back to the moment. (I would emphasize to inexperienced meditators that that is a perfectly valid stage of practice. You don't need to have developed perfect mindfulness to deal with difficult mind states.) This process went on for an indeterminate length of time. It might have been a half hour, might have been an hour and a half.

When nausea came up, I couldn't at first be mindful of it. I would repeat the word *Buddho* to myself, keying it to the breathing like a mantra, and the nausea would fall away. But when I dropped the word it returned.

Finally attention became unwavering. There were no more attempts at escape or lapses into self-preoccupation. There was complete intimacy with the energy of fear, observation without the separation of a self-conscious observer. In the light of that awareness my nausea fell away; it seemed to have been totally a function of the fear. After a long period like that—again, I don't know how long—everything broke apart. The terrifying images disappeared. I had a long period of weeping, followed by a deep feeling of peace.

Things really changed for me after that day. It was clear that my earlier interests had been what psychotherapists refer to as counterphobic: I had taken an intellectual interest in the Holocaust out of a deeply buried fear. I no longer had my obsessive interest in the Nazis after that afternoon at IMS, and there was much more peace in my life.

I also found that once I'd had that profound encounter with a major emotion, the skill I'd used became transferable, and I was better able to work with other negative emotions. I had seen that even that extremely elaborate fear was just a form of energy in motion—strong body sensations and disabling thoughts—and that when I didn't identify with it I was much more able to deal with it.

Attachment can be craving or pushing away; either way, it causes suffering. When we learn to stop attaching, we can be with life as it is in the moment and let it go when the time comes to do that. Clear seeing is a form of intelligence. It is unintelligent to try to hold on to things, to freeze them, when we can't.

The truth is that we don't own anything, not our bodies, not even the content of our minds. That's actually good news (though not for the ego: it immediately compensates by resolving to be a great practitioner, really to see through itself and become a famous meditator). Wisdom has helped us let go of the burden of attaching to things as me or mine. We are able to lay that burden down.

I remember an image I saw about this truth in Japan. It was a cartoon of a Zen monk walking along the beach carrying a huge sack. It was so heavy that his footsteps were like craters. On the sack it said ME. That's the burden we need to lay down. It will make our life incomparably lighter.

THE CROWN JEWEL

In English we translate the Pali word *vipassana* as insight, and the practice that I teach, in the Theravada tradition, has come to be known in this country as Insight meditation. When the Insight Meditation Society was founded, and when I started the Cambridge Insight Meditation Center, we chose to use the English word *insight* instead of the Pali—*vipassana*—because we felt the foreign word would alienate people.

The problem is that the English word *insight* has various meanings, and people sometimes think it refers to the kinds of insight that people have in therapy or dream analysis or journal writing. Such insights do show up in meditation and can be extremely valuable. But *vipassana* has a very specific meaning, and refers to the wisdom specified in these last four contemplations. To see impermanence is to see all of it.

The thirteenth contemplation asks us to become intimate with impermanence in the same way that, in the first two contemplations, we grew intimate with the breathing. Such knowing involves not thinking but sensitive looking, allowing whatever you contemplate to come and tell you what it is. This level of contemplation can go very deep, to a point beyond all our understandings, where even an attempt to put it into words makes no sense. At that deep place, anicca and dukkha and anatta are all the same thing. Suffering and not-self are a part of impermanence the way heat and color are a part of fire.

At whatever level you want to look—from microscopic to cosmic—everything is in constant flux. That leads to a great deal of uncertainty, which people sometimes find overwhelming. When there is a natural disaster like a hurricane or an earthquake, or a personal disaster like sudden illness, these things definitely cause suffering, but seen in another way they are just a reflection of the way things are always changing. It's nothing personal, the universe might say.

I have best been able to see this principle on long retreats, where the deep subtlety of change is apparent, and everything is becoming something else, endlessly. You listen to your consciousness, and thoughts come and go without end. They are not consistent or in harmony with each other. They're not governable and not predictable. They just appear and disappear, like clouds in the sky. To see this process is to see emptiness.

Emptiness is the crown jewel of Buddhism. If everything is constantly changing, then nothing has a substantial core with any degree of endurance. Some things last longer than others, of course. And change isn't always unpleasant. When pain departs, that's good.

It is important, however, that you not accept these teachings merely on faith. Often people get involved with a Buddhist community and receive some benefit—a degree of calm, perhaps—along with a new group of friends and a whole new set of books to read. They hear that everything is empty and want to agree with that, because they belong to the group. They become attached to that belief, and the attachment causes suffering.

We shouldn't equate ultimate truth with a belief. We hear the principles, certainly, but then look at our experience to see if they are true. We just need enough faith to investigate.

The real work is to look, listen, and learn. Every one of us must do this work for ourselves, find the liberating power of seeing that the self is an illusion, really seeing that the way you would anything else, directly, clearly, and more than once, sometimes with a profound and convincing energy that changes you forever. It's actually wonderful to see that you're nobody and that all the fear you've had all your life was in relation to this self you thought you had. You have one less thing to promote, protect, maintain, dress up, and present to the world.

In any case, in Buddhist thought, these three facets of experience are inextricably linked: anicca (impermanence), dukkha (suffering, a basic unsatisfactoriness to life), and anatta (emptiness of self). These are the three signata of Buddhism, the royal stamp. Without insight into this cluster of concepts, what you are seeing in practice may be interesting, and may be quite valuable, but it is not Buddha dharma.

Let me speak of one practical way to examine anatta. This is an advanced practice, so let's imagine that you're on a three-month retreat, one devoted specifically to the *Anapanasati Sutra*. The whole point is to notice things you haven't previously, so you start with the simplest one, the breathing, which has been with you all your life. From that you move rather naturally into the body, because the breathing takes place there, and become familiar with it in a new way, as if it's a vast mansion that you're slowly exploring.

In the body you begin to notice sensations—aching knees, aching back—as well as, eventually, deep feelings of peace from sitting still and being with the breathing. In that peace you notice the mind, which early in the retreat seemed a distraction from these processes, but which now that you've achieved some calm can be an object of contemplation itself. You see the vast, fascinating, ever changing process we call the mind.

Then your teacher says, "It's time to practice vipassana."

At that stage in the retreat, you have gotten to a place where your samadhi is strong and reliable. You can usually just call upon it and get calm and concentrated at will. Perhaps that is possible for you now, through years of practice, though it might not take years; some people learn it quite quickly. You sit and are aware of the breathing, but not in a pinpoint way. Your attention is not at the nostrils or chest or abdomen but, in a much more open way, on the whole body, a panoramic view of the sitting breathing body.

It is possible to come to a place where you contemplate this breathing body, and there is no question that breathing is happening, but at the same time you can't find a breather. That can be a wonderful feeling, because the breather is just an ego disguised as a meditator. The breather has a nice spiritual look, the right clothes and right posture, but there's a self-consciousness about the breather, a sense of someone trying to meditate correctly.

When that disappears, there's just the innocence of a body sitting there breathing and knowing that it is.

That is what happened to me that afternoon with Ajahn Buddhadasa, the teacher who taught me so much about this practice and this sutra. There was a moment when he said, "Can you find a breather?" and I said no. He said, "So I guess there isn't one," and I said, "Wait a minute. I'm the breather." He said, "That's just a thought."

When you look with the light of awareness, the self falls away. The body's just sitting and breathing. There's a feeling of being breathed, rather than of breathing to attain anything. You see that the body can sit and breathe in a tremendous state of fulfillment and doesn't need a self to do that.

People sometimes get confused about the doctrine of anatta, thinking it means that there isn't a body. The Buddha isn't saying that. Clearly, there is a body, and while we're here our moments are composed of life in this physical form. The Buddha's is a balanced view. You don't get caught up in identifying with the body, in romanticizing it, and you don't get caught up in denying it either.

It is when we identify with the body too much that we suffer. Let's say—on this imaginary retreat—you feel a pain in your knee. There isn't much mindfulness, and you identify with the pain. My knee is killing me! You go to your teacher, who says, "Try to be sensitive to the sensations in the knee. Just observe them." That sense of self falls away, and often the pain diminishes. Then there's a lapse of attention—it doesn't take much— and the pain flares up again. Again you give your attention to it.

You can investigate the whole phenomenon and thereby notice that the pain is not you; it's a natural process that is happening to the body because of certain conditions. This is a practical matter: it helps you in life when you don't identify the body as self.

It's the same with feelings and mind states. Let's say that on this retreat you have a sitting before lunch in which the mind is very still; there's almost no thought at all. The body grows peaceful and calm, and it's absolutely effortless to observe the breathing. You drift out of the meditation hall thinking what a wonderful meditator you are, almost floating on air. In that blissed-out state—maybe you want to celebrate a little—you eat more lunch than usual. It's also one of those rare occasions when cookies are served. You eat three.

Suddenly after lunch you have a very full feeling, and you've had problems with your weight in the past, so that feeling makes you feel fat. You trudge back to your room feeling like the Pillsbury Doughboy. Your stomach hurts and your pants feel tight. "I haven't changed a bit," you think. "I'm not a meditator at all."

If you go to your teacher on this occasion, the teacher will let you know that to attach to any feelings, either of the body or of the mind, is wrong understanding. You've created a sense that the whole thing is happening to you. First you identified with the good feelings, and that reminded you of your self-image as a good meditator; then you identified with the bad ones, and that brought up the memory of an unhappy overweight childhood.

But those feelings are just feelings, your self-image and your memory are just perceptions and labels. They're not you. To do this contemplation on anatta would be to see that a thought is just a thought. You don't deny that you had the feelings and thoughts, but you don't make them into self.

None of this makes sense unless you see that that is a wise way to be. It isn't that you're trying to be a Buddha or a part of the sangha. It's that you're no longer creating self. You thereby make your life lighter.

Wisdom is the art of living happily. Much of that art comes from seeing how we live unhappily. The notion of anatta is not meant to be subscribed to as a philosophical belief. It is a method of looking carefully at who you think you are and what you think you're doing. And thereby seeing who you really are.

EMPTYING THE MIND

When you stop identifying with things as self, you don't suddenly disappear. You don't walk around feeling vague or lost. You actually feel more alive than ever, more focused and intelligent, though your intelligence isn't based on knowledge acquired over time. Emptiness has the ability to know. When the mind is clear and empty, it is much more trustworthy in terms of what it sees and the actions that come out of that seeing.

The teaching on not-self can also be examined in light of the mind, where we take a look at our old friends the kilesas: greed, hatred, and delusion. We might, for example, be sitting and notice that greed arises in the mind. The fact that it does is out of our control; it arises and departs when it wants. Typically, it propels us into action, often some foolish action, because we overestimate the object that we want. We thereby find ourselves suffering.

But the reason our greed is so powerful is that we identify with it. We regard our particular need as part of a self. The energy takes us over, and when we emerge, we find we've done something we regret. With practice, we develop the capacity to examine craving as a phenomenon. We're not repressing it, but we're also not getting lost or drowning in it. We see it for what it is.

It is important not to get caught in either of these extremes. Often when people begin spiritual practice, they hear that craving is a problem, and they want not to have that problem, so when craving comes up they repress it. That never works. The craving keeps returning until it is felt. The way of practice is to examine craving in the light of awareness. We're learning the art of unconditional opening. It is in this openness that our practice—liberation through nonclinging—can flower.

When you open to a mind state in that way and fully experience it, the identification with it—the tendency to make self out of it—is short-circuited. Identification with an object cannot coexist with real awareness of it. When you're fully aware of a mind state—the same way you're aware of the breathing—you'll see that it's just there. It doesn't belong to anyone.

So, to practice with the contemplation of not-self, you sit and breathe, with some amount of composure and clarity. You see the mind wanting, wanting, wanting, but you don't identify with the wanting and create a self. You just see it, see that it lacks a core, and stop attaching to it. Either that, or you do attach, and watch yourself get burned. Either of these is a valuable practice. We can't regulate what comes into our consciousness. All we can do is relate to it in a new way.

There is a huge literature on the mind. The Buddha himself gave many talks on it, and through the centuries a great many other extraordinary masters have also described their experience of meditation. It is fine to read that literature—much of it is inspiring—but ultimately we have to look into our own mind and see its truths for ourselves. It doesn't help us that the Buddha got free unless we can use his teachings to free ourselves.

The Buddha was with his followers at one point and picked up a handful of leaves. "Are there more leaves in the forest or in my hand?" he asked. They said that of course there were more in the forest. "What I know is the equivalent of the whole forest," he said. "What I'm teaching you is the amount in my hand. Just the essentials. Enough to liberate you from suffering."

What the Buddha had in his hand can be summed up by the teaching we've already mentioned: under no circumstances attach to anything as me or mine. If you've heard those words, you've heard all of the Buddha's teachings. If you've put them into practice, you've practiced his teachings. If you've tasted their fruit, you've tasted the fruit of his teachings.

And at the heart of those words is the concept we've been talking about: emptiness, or not-self. The word in Pali is *sunnata,* and the Buddha said he lived in *sunnata vihara,* the house of emptiness. That was the place from which he taught. In other words, his mind was empty.

All of us are actually empty in the way that the Buddha was. We don't have to change anything. The problem is that we don't see it. Our minds seem anything but empty. We have a continuous flow of notions about who we are, who we used to be, who we will be, and we take these mental conditions to be self. We have the same kinds of notions about other people. That's why our personal relations are such a mess; images are encountering other images. When our images are assaulted, we suffer.

In the West we tend to think that images have real importance and that fulfillment involves changing them. You move from a poor self-image on to a good one, then—no doubt—to a superb one. You're moving from a nightmare to a happy dream. From the point of view of practice, all of these images are equal, and they're all equally false. If you stay with the practice long enough, all your images, even the cherished ones, will be shattered. You'll give up the dream altogether. You'll wake up.

We think that the way to happiness is by strengthening the self, making it feel more confident, getting it more money, giving it more prestige, making it physically attractive. The practice isn't against any of those things per se. But if you make them into self, you suffer.

At one point the Buddha says, "Birth is suffering." There are various levels of meaning to that statement. Obviously, there is suffering in the physical process of birth. Also, once the body comes into existence, it is liable to all the kinds of suffering that we've been talking about. But there is also a more subtle level to these words. Suffering arises through the birth of the ego. All day long the ego is born and passes away, every time a situation gives a new sense of "me."

Such suffering can happen to anyone. It can happen to a street person, for instance, not merely from the fact that the person is cold, unprotected, doesn't have enough food—all the obvious things—but also that the person identifies with the situation: I'm no good. I'm worthless. I'm a bum. There is also the suffering of the wealthy. In the Great Depression, there were people so identified with their bankbooks that, when they lost their money, they committed suicide.

I once knew a Canadian monk in Thailand. He seemed an impeccable monk from the outside, but he confessed to me that he was extremely unhappy. The problem was that all through the day he kept being bombarded by the thought, "I'm a monk. I'm a monk."

Sometimes that self-image made him pleased with himself, when he thought he was living up to it. Other times he was tormented by the thought that he was failing it. Either way, it was a burden.

If a man were going to Wall Street every day in an expensive suit, Italian shoes, the finest overcoat money could buy, and he was just dressing that way because it was a convention, he didn't think it identified him at all, he would be freer than the monk, though the monk was wearing humble robes. Monastic life hadn't freed that man. It had become one more trap.

The final question of this practice, and of all spiritual life, is, Who are you? At the beginning you answer with conventional ideas about yourself. But as you look at them carefully, they don't stand up. They come and go, empty of an essential core. As they fade away, you come into contact with something that has tremendous depth and space, that is very alive. It's a vast extraordinary space that can be lived in and from, but it is unnameable. As soon as you name it—and the ego gets hold of it—it shrinks. You're just a small person once again.

The message of this practice is liberation. And although it seems to concern individuals, it is not necessarily selfish, though it might be that way at first. The self with all its wants is the problem. If you mature with practice further, you'll see that you're practicing not for yourself but for all beings. We all have the same mind, and if you develop more clarity and sanity, you help everyone.

PRACTICING WITH EMPTINESS

It might be helpful at this point in the sutra to take another look at the process of observation. Mindfulness—just attending to our experience in this moment—is basic to all practices in Buddhism, and it typically goes through various stages. At first the attempt to observe comes out of our conditioning as, for example, an American in this culture, with our own life experiences and accomplishments. It is difficult to get disentangled from them.

When we're observing from our psyche, we're motivated by self-interest. We therefore don't reflect whatever arises like a clear mirror, which has no investment in what it's seeing. As the practice unfolds, that starts to change, and we begin to have moments when we are not observing from a particular point of view.

At that point, you might be disentangled from your psychological predispositions, but there's still a self-consciousness. There's someone who's *doing* this activity, therefore a certain separation and distortion. That's natural when you're learning something new. It's like riding a bicycle. At first there's an awkward feeling of being on top of this weird contraption, trying to keep your balance, but in time that falls away and you're just riding.

If you practice long enough, a day comes when feelings of self-consciousness disappear. The mind gets silent, with effortless alertness. The observer falls away. There is no separation from the object. You're not trying to pay attention; you're just doing it. There is only attention.

When the observer is present, that is the feeling of me or mine. *Trying* to meditate, in spite of the observer, involves suffering. Often people come to interviews and say, "I want my practice to be better. I should be calmer by now. I want to start having these insights you keep talking about. I don't know what they are but I want to have them."

It's the observer who's suffering, the ego dressed up as a yogi, and he's got a ripe new field. It's not money, sex, or power. It's something he suddenly sees as more important than any of these. Spiritual practice! We turn the process of observation into a backbreaking task. We make our meditation space into a torture chamber and create within the practice the very suffering that we came to get rid of. On the day when you see you're doing that—it's actually quite freeing—the practice becomes much lighter and more joyful.

During a retreat at the Insight Meditation Society a few years ago, they were doing renovations on one of the buildings, so that instead of the idyllic sounds of springtime—birds chirping and squirrels chattering—there were sounds of power saws and hammering and lumber being tossed around. All the meditators had been warned, but they still arrived with a certain expectation about the retreat—as a place of silence and peace—and found themselves instead at a construction site. People would come to interviews. "When is this noise going to stop? It's driving me crazy. I can't meditate."

The truth of the matter—as we said back in the second chapter—is that meditation is always dealing with simple sensations. They were supposed to be *chirp chirp* but instead were *bang bang*, or the grinding buzz of a power saw. No matter what the sound, it is really just vibrations hitting a sense organ. It is pleasant, unpleasant, or neutral, and there is nothing wrong with perceiving hammering and sawing as unpleasant.

In practicing this contemplation on emptiness, you would leave it right there. You wouldn't take the next step, which takes "sound" and makes it "noise" (which involves a judgment). You also wouldn't take the further step: "How can they do this to me? This was supposed to be a meditation retreat. I'm paying good money to be here." Or maybe you would take those steps, but you'd see yourself take them. You'd watch yourself create suffering out of a simple sense perception.

It isn't feelings we're trying to avoid but their proliferation into something else. Even if they do proliferate, and you give birth to all these different people, you'll at least see that there isn't a substantial self. You're just a series of births and deaths happening, all day long. You're a process.

Through the years, teachers in various traditions have expressed this truth. One of my favorites is from the great Chinese poet Li Po.

> The birds have vanished into the sky,
> And now the last cloud drains away.
> We sit together, the mountain and me,
> Until only the mountain remains.

He is speaking of the experience of emptiness, during which the object you're observing—in his case a mountain—becomes all the more magnificent. Depending on the intensity and duration of your "absence," it could become an enlightenment experience. It could change the observer's life forever.

Another useful teaching is from the Christian tradition: "It is easier for a camel to go through the eye of a needle than for a rich man to enter the Kingdom of God." I have never thought that quotation meant there is anything wrong with wealth and riches. Wealth is just like anything else. You can have it and not be attached, so it's not a problem, or you can identify it as yours, and it becomes the object of great suffering.

This saying of Jesus' might just reflect how difficult it is not to attach to wealth; when you have a great deal, it's hard not to believe it's you. But I think that at a more subtle level, he was referring to the ego. When the ego is rich and identifies with all kinds of things, it can't enter the Kingdom of Heaven. When you drop all of that, the kingdom is right there. You're already in it.

Another excellent teaching on this subject is from Zen master Lin Chi, who coined the term *true person of no rank*. That phrase expresses this whole teaching for me. You could be the CEO of the largest corporation in the world and it wouldn't fundamentally change you. You could be a janitor in the most dismal building in the world and that wouldn't either.

The true person of no rank doesn't feel superior to others. He or she doesn't feel inferior, and doesn't feel equal. The whole system of ranking just isn't a part of the person's consciousness. It has no meaning.

OLD DHARMAS NEVER DIE

Korean teachers sometimes use an image that expresses the emptiness of self. They spoke of an abandoned tropical island, where we have been told someone is living. We search and search, cover the place from top to bottom. Finally we realize no one is there. At that moment, we notice that the island is extraordinarily beautiful.

This image expresses the deepest meaning of the word *delusion*. We honestly believe there is a solid self that is in control. The practice doesn't ask us to believe something different. It just suggests that we take a look around the island. See if we can find someone.

It doesn't really help to accept emptiness as an idea. It only helps to see it: that everything is impermanent, everything is interrelated, nothing is substantial, we're all conditions for one another. The *Hua-yen Sutra* expresses this truth by saying that if we remove even a single mote of dust from the universe, the whole thing will fall apart.

The fourteenth contemplation follows naturally out of our understanding of emptiness.

> 14. One trains oneself: "Focusing on fading away, I breathe in. Focusing on fading away, I breathe out."

This contemplation is possible only when your mind has become quite calm and clear, your ability to concentrate is highly developed, and you've begun to see impermanence with some depth. You've learned to look into all three areas we've discussed, the body, the feelings, and the mind. Everywhere you look, the formations that arise pass away.

They don't obey our wishes; they obey some law that doesn't ask our approval. As the mind becomes still, you clearly see the moments of coming and going. Once again, you see that all dharmas are empty, which doesn't mean they are worthless. It means they are not solid in the way we thought they were.

The fourteenth contemplation has tremendous practical significance. What is really fading is our attachment to things. As you come to see the lawfulness of arising and passing away—see it not with your brain but with the marrow of your bones—letting go starts to happen naturally. It doesn't make sense to hold on to something in a field where constant dynamic change is so vivid and apparent.

Some people object that this aspect of the practice isn't realistic. "We have relationships," they say. "We have marriages. We have children. Of course there's attachment. We don't want to give that up." I encourage them to reflect on the distinction between love and attachment. I do think it's possible to eliminate the ache of attachment, which is not the same thing as love, though people often confuse the two.

More and more, as we see the law of impermanence at work, a different kind of intelligence is born, an organic intelligence that is prior to thinking. We don't often tap into it, we're so busy with our thoughts. But there is far more to human consciousness than we've been led to believe. Its real jewels are buried.

You can practice this contemplation in terms of the body. As you sit breathing in and out, gradually calming down and achieving a certain stillness, you see that the body is alive. It's not solid; it is energy in a state of constant change. Sometimes the way the energy is aggregated feels pleasant; other times it is painful. However it is, that state arises, then passes away. Our attachment fades with it.

You can do the same practice with feelings, which are slightly more subtle than body formations, but whether pleasant, unpleasant, or neutral, they all pass away. Mind states are still more difficult to observe. We're also much more attached to them.

We are deeply attached, for instance, to what we think of as our story. We all have one, and we love to tell it. If we have no one else, we tell it to ourselves, all day long. Something new happens and we immediately fit it in, make it another example of the same old thing.

But as you begin to see thoughts as formations, and to observe them—just as you do bodily formations—you see that they're quite mechanical. They're extraordinarily repetitive. We go over the same old conversations again and again, keep inventing new ones that will never happen. We have well-worn ruts in our brains.

They're conditioned by our culture and by our personal history. Many of them come right out of things we've been told by our parents and teachers.

We nevertheless take tremendous pride in our thoughts and give them great authority in our lives. It wouldn't be an exaggeration to say that we worship thought. Buddhist, Christian, Jewish, Islamic, scientific, personal: all of these forms of thought have tremendous influence over us. We are virtually enslaved to them.

Yet they are just thoughts. They arise and pass away and have no more reality than a sound we hear or a pain in our leg. Once you see that, your passion for thought begins to fade away. You can see when it is called for, see when it is helpful, and otherwise drop it. This isn't to discredit the many marvels created by thought. It is to put it in its proper place.

When you get to the point where you're ready for the fourteenth contemplation, you've watched the mind a great deal, seen the same old thoughts come up again and again, and you don't rise to the bait anymore. It's like seeing *Gone with the Wind* for the fifth time, or the twelfth, however many it takes you. The first eleven were great, but the twelfth doesn't work anymore. You just don't care. The same thing happens with the movie in your mind, if you really start to watch it.

All of the products of mind—fear, hatred, love, envy, greed, compassion, anxiety, tenderness—come and go. When we're attached, we want them to last longer than they do or leave before they do, but as we watch the law of impermanence, we see that our wishes are futile. You can't get a grip on a waterfall. Our observation of this truth comes to resemble that of any other natural phenomenon. There is a certain joy in seeing lawfulness unfold.

That is the strength of good samadhi, the stillness that can come with practice. It makes the mind much more sensitive. Such stillness is charged with life. You're more alive when you enter into it and more intelligent when you come out. You see something you've seen a million times and it's as if for the first time.

Early on in the practice, there is inevitably some conceptualization mixed in with this seeing. Such deep seeing takes years of practice, and in the meantime you've heard the concepts a million times. That's not a problem. Little by little the process gets purified, and finally you see things as they are, not mixed in with your history or with what you've learned. As you do that, your attachments weaken. It's not something you have to try. It just happens.

Ajahn Chah saw what a great hurry Westerners were in to let go and encouraged them to slow down. He felt that you couldn't let go until you had really observed your attachment. Once you've gotten to know it, he said, much of the battle is won.

So the thirteenth contemplation quite naturally becomes the fourteenth; as you see that things are impermanent, your attachment to them fades away just as ripe fruit falls from a tree. It sometimes happens very quickly. Other times it might take years. But that gradual fading takes the ache out of it. Our suffering is slowly relieved.

THE CESSATION OF SUFFERING

The last four contemplations are like a slow-motion movie. In actual practice, if you have been sitting long enough to reach this point, they might happen quite rapidly, because they are almost the same thing. The Buddha slows them down to see their subtle nuances. The key to them all is number thirteen. If you see into impermanence in a profound way, the others follow quite naturally.

The key word in the fourteenth contemplation is rendered as "fading away," but the word in Pali is *viraga* and is sometimes rendered "becoming dispassionate." Your passion to cling to things, to attach to them, diminishes. The wording in the fifteenth contemplation is even more difficult. The Pali word *nirodha* is sometimes used as a synonym for nirvana. A literal translation would be "unbinding," the unbinding of the mind from greed, hatred, and delusion. It denotes the extinguishing of a fire. This contemplation has to do with cessation, which can be seen in this context as a form of liberation.

> 15. "One trains oneself: Focusing on cessation, I breathe in. Focusing on cessation, I breathe out."

This contemplation is actually just part of the intricate analysis of a process that began in the thirteenth contemplation. Seeing into impermanence, you naturally notice the fading away of attachment to all formations. In this contemplation, you see their cessation. Ajahn Buddhadasa calls it quenching, the quenching of suffering.

That quenching might in a particular case be momentary and temporary, just an end to a particular attachment; that attachment really ceases. Even in that there is a foretaste of nirvana. We begin to taste the flavor of liberation.

True liberation would be freedom from all greed, hatred, and delusion. We would be living in the world but no longer grasping at things, pushing them away, or making self out of them. Obviously, not a huge number of people attain the total cessation of a Buddha. But there is a wide range in the tasting of cessation.

It is important to understand that cessation is not annihilation. Early in our practice, we might confront negative states like fear, anger, loneliness, lust, and think that liberation involves annihilating them. The ego just doesn't want to be that kind of person anymore. Perhaps at the beginning we all have that wish, but there is a huge amount of self in it. And what we're imagining is not real freedom. It's just exchanging one compulsion for another.

Cessation has no self in it. It is the end of suffering, and suffering comes from attaching to things as me or mine. It is not an end to pain, of course. The body will still get sick, grow old, and die. But it is an end to the unnecessary torment that comes out of the grasping mind.

The problem, as Ajahn Chah pointed out, is that we are in such a hurry to get rid of what we don't like. Of course we dislike being filled with fear or loneliness. Those states keep us from living a full and creative life. But you can't say good-bye to something before you say hello to it. It's only good manners! It is also an empirical fact. Fear has to be allowed to arise—to emerge from consciousness—so that you can see and fully understand it before you say good-bye to it. That is what the first twelve contemplations do. They gradually introduce you to all the formations of the body, feelings, and mind.

Life gives us countless opportunities to say hello to our negative emotions, but we get little encouragement from the culture. We get a good deal of encouragement to escape, postpone, put up with, deny. The first twelve contemplations open us up to the way things are, establishing a friendly relationship with the states that terrify us. In some cases we don't even know that they do that, we've done such a good job of repressing them.

Cessation isn't just about negative states. It's about everything, allowing every formation to emerge so that we can meet it fully and intimately and watch it unfold. We don't tamper with it in any way. We come to understand it, not in an intellectual sense, but in the sense of *standing under*, really experiencing it. We see that it is impermanent, lacks an enduring core, and is not to be identified with.

We have been seeing our fear, for instance, as a huge boulder that stands in our way, but now we see that it is more like a cloud. Our attachment (which in the case of fear might be to a feeling of safety) disappears. Fear appears and we can be with it fully during its entire duration until it is gone. Seeing cessation—in the fifteenth contemplation—involves contemplating that point of going . . . and gone.

Levels of cessation depend on the depth and extent of our practice. What we've been holding on to or pushing away or confused by is allowed just to be for a time—as we're right there with it—and then to drop away. As it does, our attachment weakens. Little by little, we're not so enslaved to things.

Sometimes meditators who have been through psychotherapy

see a certain problem disappear, and they're still not satisfied. They don't feel through with it unless they can analyze it.

But the process we're learning is not an intellectual one. As I said before, often our problems are not so much *solved* in this practice as *dissolved*. They're burned up by awareness. The fading away of attachment (number fourteen) is sometimes called the path, and cessation (number fifteen) its fruition. It involves deep joy and peace, a feeling of liberation. We stop suffering because we have stopped grasping.

LETTING GO OF WHAT ISN'T THERE

The whole point of this fourth set of contemplations is to see deeply into the fact of impermanence, to see that everything is uncertain. It is the most obvious fact of human existence, but we manage to act as if everything is fixed and we know exactly what will happen. We thereby create all kinds of suffering.

One obvious example in the world today is the changes in the workforce, the downsizing of corporations. Many people in middle and upper management who thought their jobs were forever are finding out that they aren't. Various economic and historical explanations are offered, many of which are quite impressive and make a great deal of sense. But they are also just variations on a much more fundamental law, that everything changes.

You never hear that explanation on the television news, because it is so fundamental and free of content. What was unrealistic—in this larger way of looking at things—was that people thought their jobs were permanent in the first place. Nothing is permanent. There was a stable arrangement in our economy that lasted for a while—not all that long, actually—and now it is gone. That really isn't surprising. Seen from a large enough perspective, everything is changing in exactly that way, just as mysteriously. It is all just happening. We have no control.

In Buddhist education, there are three steps. The first is the one you're doing now: reading books, hearing talks, having discussions. The second is putting what you've learned into practice. If you've read every word the Buddha ever said but haven't practiced with it, it won't have much effect. Intellectual understanding in itself doesn't have much transformative power. It may be interesting and useful in a certain way, but it is limited and has little to do with the reason the words were uttered in the first place.

The third step is penetration, a deep seeing into yourself. The seeing is what brings suffering to an end, which was the whole purpose of the Buddha's teaching. He wasn't trying to be philosophical. He was eminently practical.

All of the forms of practice—sitting in silence; going on retreats where you can't talk or read or write—are really just elaborate methods of allowing you to be with yourself, to stop doing, stop trying to become something: just sit still and be as you are. It is an art. It takes sincere application and often unfolds over a long period of time. But it can eventually bear real fruit.

In the last three contemplations of this sutra we've been watching the gradual unfolding of a process that begins when you see deeply into impermanence. There is fading away, there is cessation, and finally there is letting go, which happens not because you are trying but because there is no longer anything to hold on to.

> 16. One trains oneself: "Focusing on relinquishment, I breathe in. Focusing on relinquishment, I breathe out."

What you focus on here is the process of letting go. You're not doing it, any more than you've been doing the breathing. You're just watching it happen, in an entirely natural way.

What is there to let go of? you might ask, since the fifteenth contemplation saw the cessation of the formation. But in the fourteenth and fifteenth contemplations, it is still possible for a self to be present, watching these processes and taking credit for the wise discernment that sees with such subtlety and depth. In the sixteenth, that last vestige of self disappears and there is just the seeing. You relinquish any trace of ownership and give up any clinging whatsoever, even to the practice itself.

Again, this can be a small moment or an extremely large one, all the way up to the deepest fulfillment a human being can have. This is the experience of nonclinging, not attaching to anything as me or mine. When we hear terms like *enlightenment*, or *awakening*, we think of them as way off in the future. Some people adjust to that fact and keep practicing. Others give up, if it's going to take that long.

But the practice of nonclinging is not off in the future. It is in this moment. Whatever ultimate fulfillment may be, it has to happen in this moment. The practice of liberating ourselves is an ongoing one. In any given moment, we see that we're attached to something, and that we're suffering. If we see that deeply enough, the grasping falls away and we are liberated.

We have the idea that enlightenment will be some experience of feeling good all the time. Hoping for such a state, of course, is just another kind of craving. Real enlightenment will involve being with whatever is there just the way it is, not wanting it to be another way. Or if we see ourselves wanting it another way, seeing through that wanting. It's an ongoing process.

In a sense the sixteen steps of the *Anapanasati Sutra* are a training program. You can cycle through them again and again with increasing precision and depth. You learn them as you practice through them, until you no longer need the program.

The sixteenth contemplation is where you stop grasping even the painstakingly acquired and beautifully refined tools that have brought you to where you are. The formal practice of the sixteen contemplations comes to an end, though awareness and learning continue. But it is the learning of a quiet mind, one with unhindered responsiveness to the challenges that present themselves.

All of these steps have their ultimate source in the breath. Zen master Hogen said that the whole universe is the breath. If you really pay attention to it, it takes you to its immaculate source. You can call that Buddha nature, nirvana, the deathless, whatever you want. All the names for it are human inventions. What they point to is the deepest truth we know.

5

The Condensed Method

Breathing with the
Way Things Are

> Try to be mindful, and let things take their natural
> course. Then your mind will become still in any
> surroundings, like a clear forest pool. All kinds of
> wonderful, rare animals will come to drink at the
> pool, and you will clearly see the nature of all
> things. You will see many strange and wonderful
> things come and go, but you will be still. This is
> the happiness of the Buddha.
>
> —Ajahn Chah

THE CONDENSED METHOD

One way to look at the *Anapanasati Sutra* is to see it as a
streamlined and practical version of the much longer (and not
so elegantly organized) *Satipatthana Sutra*, which is a kind of
Declaration of Independence for vipassana meditators. In the *Satipatthana Sutra*, the Buddha gives an elaborate explanation of the
Four Foundations of Mindfulness. In the *Anapanasati Sutra*, he
does the same thing by giving us four tetrads to practice with, the
four chapters we have just finished.

They end in relinquishment, which is not a giving up of anything we really owned, just a clear seeing of the way things are.

Ajahn Buddhadasa had a beautiful way of putting it: we are giving back to nature the things that we have falsely appropriated from it. This mind, these feelings, this body, the breath itself, do not really belong to us. When we see that, instead of feeling deprived of something we thought was ours, we feel a great freedom, the liberation that the Buddha promised.

The classical sixteen contemplations provide us with a wonderful course of meditative training, which leads all the way to the liberation of the sixteenth contemplation. But many sincere practitioners don't have the time or inclination to train themselves in such a systematic manner and need effective ways to practice that are more concise. Upasika Kee Nanayon, a Thai lay meditation master, condenses all four tetrads so that they can all be practiced at once.

"What we need," she says, "is a way of gathering our awareness at the breath long enough to make the mind firm, and then go straight to examining how all formations are impermanent, unsatisfactory, and not-self, so that we can see the truth of all formations with each in-and-out breath. If you can keep at this continually, without break, your mindfulness will become firm and snug enough for you to give rise to the discernment that will enable you to gain clear knowledge and vision."

Ajahn Buddhadasa, after he had outlined all sixteen steps, said that it was possible to reduce them to just two, which I think of as the condensed method:

1. Practice with the breathing until a certain level of concentration and calm is achieved.
2. Open the awareness to whatever arises in the mind-body process and see that it is all impermanent, unsatisfactory, and lacking an essential self.

This is sometimes referred to as samatha/vipassana, a two-step practice that does the work of all sixteen steps of the sutra. What turns up in consciousness will invariably be encompassed by the first twelve contemplations. The wisdom of the last four comes in as you see the impermanence of these formations and all that impermanence implies.

Another possibility is to practice the first tetrad on the body until some calm is reached, then examine any of the first three tetrads from the perspective of the fourth. This approach is a bit more structured. The meditator takes up one tetrad at a time—the body, feeling, or mind states—from the perspective of impermanence.

In the traditional method, meditators developed deep jhanic states of concentration, which begin with piti and sukha and go on to much deeper states. One school of meditation believes that you shouldn't practice vipassana at all until you have at least tasted the first jhana, a process that sometimes takes a considerable amount of time.

Another school espouses what is called moment-by-moment concentration. They say you don't need to develop jhanic states, just enough concentration to be with any object for as long as it exists, so you can see that it arises and passes away. The continuity of mindfulness is emphasized more than some deep meditative state.

My own feelings toward the *Anapanasati Sutra* have changed through the years, as I have practiced and especially as I have taught. I have not tried in this book to write a definitive commentary on it but to use it as a skillful means to launch samatha/ vipassana practice. I don't see it as *the* way, but as *a* way, and I try to be flexible in my teaching. When I encounter students who are adept at concentration practice, I encourage them to deepen it. The concentration they develop can be a powerful aid to vipassana practice.

But really to develop the jhanas usually requires an extremely rarified set of conditions. The meditator may need to be on a long retreat, protected by a great deal of silence, facing no other responsibilities in life at that moment, and guided by a skillful teacher. Such conditions aren't available for most of us. Furthermore, a Tibetan monk—Tara Tulku Rinpoche—once told me that it is difficult even for full-time contemplatives to develop the jhanas nowadays. There is a subtle level of distraction in the modern world that makes really deep concentration difficult to attain.

The way I teach is an alternative to these approaches. I don't start with vipassana from day one, but I also don't insist that meditators develop the jhanas before they observe impermanence. I give them time to develop some concentration, and I introduce vipassana once they have. The two practices develop together, complementing and strengthening each other. A calm mind can be a more insightful one; insights give rise to further calm. They grow together in an alternating rhythm.

On a nine-day retreat, I typically give the first three over to the breathing as an exclusive object, then begin with vipassana, with the understanding that some meditators will want to stay with the breath for a longer period of time.

There is no formula for how to work with the two steps of the condensed method. It will vary from person to person, retreat to retreat, sitting to sitting. One meditator was able to enter deep levels of absorption very quickly but was terrified of looking at fear, anger, and loneliness. For several years she resisted my encouragement to face such powerful energies. Eventually the day came when she was able to examine them.

Another had a difficult time getting concentrated on the breath alone but had a keen interest in his changing mind states. This interest created a natural concentration that was quite adequate to practice vipassana fruitfully. He was eventually able to do concentration practice as well.

Meditation is an art, and part of it is learning how to work with these two modes, staying with the breathing exclusively when that seems necessary, opening to a larger field of attention when it is appropriate.

It is good for all meditators to be familiar with the *Anapanasati Sutra*. Some will practice in the classical mode, moving right through the sixteen contemplations, constantly deepening their experience of each tetrad. Most will work with the condensed method. The sutra for them is an outline of what might happen as their practice unfolds and can serve as a reference text as they encounter the states of body and mind that it discusses.

To take a hard look at impermanence is to undergo a Copernican revolution, shifting the attention away from content and toward process. Most of us are fixated on content. But true vipassana practice requires us to see that it all arises and passes away. It lacks solidity. It is not real in the way we once thought. Meditators need to be somewhat at home with the content before they can do that. It can't keep startling or overwhelming them, which tends to make them cling to it or push it away. This shift from content to process is a major turning point in practice, a major advance in freedom.

So I do place value on some degree of calming. We need in this complex world to learn to appreciate a certain basic simplicity, the joy that can be found in focusing on a simple process like the breathing, but then the meditator is ready to move on to vipassana. The condensed method isn't fast food; there's nothing fast about it. It is just a different way to focus. Sooner or later, everything will come up anyway.

BECOMING CHOICELESS

The second step of the condensed method is sometimes called choiceless awareness. Once you have achieved a certain calm by following the breathing, you sit in the middle of your experience just as it is. You have no agenda regarding what to be mindful of, and you are not for or against whatever turns up.

I don't recommend this practice for beginners because it is too easy to fool yourself, to keep getting caught up in thought and believe you are practicing. But once the mind has learned to rest in the breathing and developed some stability, you open up the field to whatever is there. More and more you do less and less, until finally you're doing nothing.

As you sit in the middle of your experience, you can easily see that everything that arises passes away. Your moment-by-moment experience is extremely rich when you see it this way, just letting it come to you. You learn to let it follow its true nature, arising and disappearing.

As Yuan Wu put it, "Among the sixteen kinds of meditation, the baby's practice is the best." A baby doesn't have ideas, stories, preferences, goals. It's just there with whatever is. We quite literally don't know what will happen when we sit down on the cushion. But whatever does is all right.

In taking up the condensed method, the question inevitably confronts us: how much samatha do we need before we go on to vipassana? It is very helpful to put the *nivaranas*, the hindrances, into abeyance: sensual desire, restlessness, sloth, anger, and doubt, five states that obscure the natural radiance of the mind. That isn't to say, of course, that they will never come up again, but that the meditator will recognize them and be able to come back to the present moment.

Often when a meditator is having trouble concentrating on the breathing, it is one of these hindrances that is bothering him or her. If it keeps interrupting, it can be helpful to switch to the hindrance itself, give it the attention it is demanding while maintaining a light contact with the breathing. This isn't to think about the hindrance, or get lost in it, but to observe it with mindfulness. The breath is still in the background, of course, helping you remain attentive. When the hindrance is weakened, you can come back to the breath as an exclusive object.

Sometimes you open up to choiceless awareness and find that you keep getting lost in one mind state after another. You find yourself analyzing and psychologizing and can't stay focused. That might be a signal that it is time to go back to the breath as an exclusive object. You can fine-tune your attention with a few conscious breaths before returning to choicelessness, or finish the session with samatha practice. That doesn't mean that your practice has regressed, just that your mind is in that state at that particular moment. It's nothing to be concerned about.

Just as following the sixteen contemplations of the sutra is not necessarily superior to the condensed method, one aspect of the condensed method is not superior to the other. It is samatha/ vipassana that we are practicing, not really two steps but one unified practice. You might think of them as a right and a left hand washing each other. Neither is ever totally absent. When you're practicing vipassana, the breath is there. And when you're following the breathing, you might still see that it is impermanent. The two steps are not exclusive.

Finally, of course, it is insight that frees us, not the word but the deep seeing into impermanence that it implies.

An analogy is made in the Thai forest tradition with a spider in its web. It sits in the middle, very still, and when an insect enters the web, the spider envelopes it for nourishment. The spider is able to use whatever turns up. For the meditator, the web is the infinite reaches of the mind. The nourishment found is—similarly—whatever comes up, which one thoroughly sees, experiences, and understands. The meditator sees that each formation is impermanent, not ultimately fulfilling, and lacking in an essential core. This helps us develop a certain disenchantment, a lack of fixation, an ease of letting go.

For long periods of time—like the spider—you might sit in silence. That is not wasted time. The silence is also nourishing. What we are learning to rest in finally is awareness itself, Buddho: that which knows. All the arising and passing away, and the growing periods of silence, are the contemplative's food.

The attitude to sit with is one of total receptivity and openness. You lay the calculating mind to rest and allow life to come to you, without reaching out for anything at all. You sit with relaxed alertness, knowing that life will provide you with all the material necessary for your meditation to flourish. Whatever is there is perfect to practice with, because it is there. It is your life in that moment.

The breathing might be alongside what you're observing, providing a kind of support. Sometimes, especially after you've practiced for a while, it blends in with what you're observing, which can be very helpful, especially when you're confronting difficult states like fear, loneliness, or anger. The awareness of breathing and what is being attended to are experienced as a unified field. Calm and insight are literally developing simultaneously.

When we first try to practice choiceless awareness, there is a certain self-consciousness involved, a bit of effort. We don't have much experience of doing nothing, and it takes time to settle into it. In true choiceless awareness—which develops after a while—there is no effort whatsoever.

It is like the distinction sometimes made between mindfulness and awareness. Mindfulness involves conscious effort; it is something you can practice. But it is moving toward real awareness, which is utterly without effort. Even the breath is no longer important in the depths of awareness and doesn't need to occupy a special place. It is one more impermanent phenomenon like any other. You might notice it for a while, but you don't need to keep coming back to it.

The two steps of the condensed method are illustrated by a famous teaching story from India. There was a king who lived in a large magnificent palace and was known to be enlightened. So a spiritual aspirant came to him and asked how he too might achieve enlightenment. The king said, "Take a bucket, fill it with hot oil, balance it on your head, and walk around the whole palace without spilling a drop."

This was a daunting task, and there was much to practice. First the young man had to learn to balance something on his head, then to walk carefully, then to balance the bucket itself. He practiced with water in the bucket, then with hot water, finally with oil. He had many trials and tribulations, but eventually a day came when he walked around the entire palace with a bucket of hot oil on his head and didn't spill a drop. He hurried to the king with great excitement.

"That's great," the king said. "By the way, what's going on around the palace? Any gossip? Affairs? Intrigues?"

The young man said he hadn't noticed. He'd been concentrating too hard on the bucket of oil.

"All right," the king said. "Now walk back around the palace with a bucket of hot oil on your head and notice what's happening. Then come back and report to me."

The breathing is our bucket of hot oil. It keeps us in the present moment and helps us retain our clarity and attention. But the real point is to be aware of what is happening, in the palace of our body, the palace of our mind, the palace of the whole world. The breathing is intended as an aid for that, not just for periods of sitting, but for our entire lives. We're learning to pay attention to our lives. That is the point of practice. The breath is a gateway into all that is other than breath.

One of my students tells the story that, in a practice group one evening, while they were sitting, I suggested that they try to spend five minutes in which they didn't move at all. That sounded difficult to him—he'd only been practicing for about a year and a half—but it was just for five minutes, so he put every bit of effort he had into it.

The results, alas, were comical. The instruction not to move meant that he didn't correct his posture, not that he didn't get tired, so his posture gradually crumpled in the course of the five minutes. Probably all the effort he was expending made him more tired than he would normally have been. By the time five minutes were up, he was practically horizontal.

At the end of that same practice period, in the last five minutes, I said, "Okay, now I want you to stop meditating. Stay in your posture, stay on your cushion, but just sit there." All evening he'd been straining to sit in position, trying to follow the breathing. Now he stopped and just sat. He found it rather easy. Furthermore, even though he wasn't trying to, he kept noticing the breathing. He couldn't seem to get his mind off it.

There was a lesson in that for him. There is a lesson for all of us. It is often our very trying that is getting in the way. What we're learning is surrender, to the breathing, to the body, to life just as it is, and the way we get there is not by *trying* to surrender—that's a contradiction in terms—but by ceasing to try. We accept ourselves just as we are, where we are. If we feel ourselves trying, we notice that. Our attention will take care of it in time. Our attention takes care of everything.

The consummation of choiceless awareness, to my mind, is "just sitting," letting go of all supports, methods, directions, techniques, and just being there, with awareness. We come to each moment empty-handed, just being ourselves without pretense. There is no control, no conflict, no reaching out, no searching or waiting. We let each moment come forward and tell its story, not necessarily in words. We stop trying to figure everything out; just being ourselves is the practice.

When I first went to Korea with my teacher Soen Sunim, he took us all around the country and showed us Buddha images in different temples. Finally one day he said, "Today I'm going to show you what everyone agrees is the most beautiful image of the Buddha in all of Korea." I was quite excited because I cherish images of the Buddha. But the temple was up on a high mountain, and it was pouring rain, so we had a very difficult journey for five or six hours. It was hard to walk, and we kept slipping and falling in the mud.

Finally we got to the top and went into the temple to sit, and it was simply a large, clear space. There was only a small sign above the altar where the statue of the Buddha usually is. We were disappointed, and asked our teacher what the sign said. He read it to us: "If you can't see the Buddha on this altar, you had better go back down the hill and practice some more." That was very liberating. It let us know not to look for anything. When you're looking for something, you miss what is there.

6

Breathing with Daily Life

There are no mundane things outside of Buddhism, and there is no Buddhism outside of mundane things."

—Yuan-Wu

PRACTICE IS EVERY MOMENT

One of my favorite Buddhist teachings is a deadpan exchange between the Venerable Webu Sayadaw of Burma and one of his students:

Sayadaw: Don't all of you breathe in and out?

Student: We do breathe, sir.

Sayadaw: When do you start breathing in and out?

Student: When we are born, sir.

Sayadaw: Do you breathe in and out when you sit upright?

Student: Yes, sir.

Sayadaw: When you are walking?

Student: We do breathe in and out then also, sir.

Sayadaw: Do you breathe when you are eating, drinking, and working to make a living?

Student: Yes, sir.

Sayadaw: Do you breathe when you go to sleep?

Student: Yes, sir.

Sayadaw: Are there times when you are so busy that you have to say, "Sorry, I have no time to breathe now, I am too busy"?

Student: There isn't anybody who can live without breathing, sir.

When I teach beginners, I try from the start to give them some idea of the larger scope of practice that Webu Sayadaw is referring to here. The first class always focuses on the sitting posture, on the simple but profound act of following the breathing. I also give instructions in walking meditation, which is neglected by some meditators but is a vital part of the practice. And before students leave at the end of the session, I give them at least some instruction on taking the practice into daily life.

All of that can be quite overwhelming. First they discover how difficult it is to sit and follow the breathing, then I tell them they have to follow it also when they're walking, and finally, as they are about to head out the door, I tell them they should actually be following it all day long. Just follow every breath from now until you come back for the next class. Have a good week!

But this larger perspective is quite necessary, and it is important to maintain it from the start. We all tend to associate Buddhism with sitting practice. Most statues of the Buddha show him sitting; they don't show him chopping vegetables in the kitchen or cleaning up the meditation hall. But though these icons portray sitting practice, we can't make sitting practice into an icon. We can't equate sitting with practice.

The Buddha himself said that it was necessary to develop mindfulness in all four postures, sitting, standing, walking, and lying down. Really he was using a kind of shorthand with these words. He meant that we need to develop mindfulness in every aspect of our lives.

The Buddha was once asked why his monks looked so serene and radiant. He replied, "They do not lament the past nor crave for things in the future, but maintain themselves"—that is the crucial phrase—"in whatever comes. Therefore they are serene."

He wasn't talking just about sitting practice. He was talking about the way his monks maintained themselves all day long. In anapa-nasati—the way of the full awareness with breathing—we make awareness of breathing a part of this day-long practice.

The often-heard complaint (especially in the modern world) that people don't have time for meditation practice relates to a fundamental misunderstanding. What people mean is that they don't have time to sit, which may or may not be true. They feel that way because they haven't established the true value of sitting. Once they do, they are much more likely to find time for it.

But practice isn't just about sitting and has nothing to do with finding time. Practice is for every moment of your life. Wherever you are, whatever your circumstance, whatever your mental state, that is a perfect moment for practice. As Dogen wrote, "If you want to attain suchness, you should practice suchness without delay."

I was introduced to this way of practice by my first Buddhist teacher, Zen Master Seung Sahn. We were taught when we were in the meditation hall to give ourselves 100 percent to the sitting. When we came out and it was time to do the dishes, we were to do that task in the same way. We weren't to separate such activities in our minds. We were to treat our lives as one seamless web.

I don't want to pretend that sitting isn't special. It is the place where we have intentionally limited our responsibilities so that we can be with ourselves as we are. We are not talking, eating, working. We are not using our bodies to go somewhere or do something. Even thinking is toppled from its lofty position of authority and seen as just one more phenomenon over which we have no control. We simply sit and get to know ourselves as we are.

At the same time, sitting isn't special at all. It—like anything else—will cause suffering if we cling to it too tightly.

In its worst form, this emphasis on formal practice can become almost pathological. Typically, people come to practice because they have been wounded by life. We have all been wounded, and that is certainly nothing to be ashamed of. But people who are drawn to practice see it as a way to heal their wounds. In sitting, in day-long sittings, in nine-day and even three-month retreats, they find a soothing balm for their pain. In the battle of life, the meditation center becomes a field hospital.

Yet there are certain kinds of people who try to make the field hospital their permanent dwelling. The only time they are really alive and happy is on retreat. All they talk about away from the meditation center is the last retreat they were on, or the next one they are planning. They stay away just long enough to earn the money to get back. Their whole focus is on formal practice. They become a rarified kind of nonhospitalizable schizophrenic.

From a certain standpoint, these people are real practitioners, devoted meditators. But to me they are missing the whole point. If I am the attending physician in the field hospital, I understand that people need time to heal their wounds. But at some point, it is my job to get them back into the fray. It is life that is the real teacher. Practice should open us to a fuller life, not cut us off from it altogether.

The intention of the Cambridge Insight Meditation Center was to address this very problem right from the start. I had seen countless people go on retreat at the Insight Meditation Society, where, no matter how long they stayed, everything was done for them. Meals were cooked, bells were rung to announce the schedule, the meditation hall was kept silent. Everything was a gigantic stage set for their immersion in consciousness.

Then they came back to Cambridge and boom!—they were right back in the midst of the insanity. It was one situation or the other, with no way to integrate the two. A number of us wanted to create a center in the midst of the insanity, a place where you could enter into formal practice for brief periods—a day or a weekend—and return promptly to your other activities. We wanted formal practice to be less separate from daily life.

All Dharma teachers encourage their students to take the practice into daily life, but unless we are careful, that instruction just becomes a cliché that students promptly ignore. Sitting and formal practice and going on retreats are Buddhism. Taking out the garbage and looking after your child and going to work are just life. Yet if you give some attention to how much time you spend in these different activities, you see how backward that is. However dedicated you are, you still spend much more time off the cushion than on it.

In that way, it is wrong to call what we do—trying to stay with the breath from moment to moment throughout the day—practice, which sounds artificial and contrived. It is really a way of living, one in which we give attentiveness and alertness to every moment the highest priority. Finally it is not a technique or practice at all. It is much larger than that.

I don't feel that going out to the kitchen to cook my dinner is inferior to sitting. Talking to my wife is certainly not inferior. Going to the bathroom is not inferior. These things are all just life in that moment. Look with naive eyes and you will see that life is just one such thing after another. Practice isn't a part of life. Practice is life. And life is practice.

That is the wonderful thing about the breathing, and the reason it is such a helpful object of attention. It is both perfectly ordinary (we are all doing it, all the time) and extremely special (if we weren't doing it, we'd be dead). There is nothing Buddhist about it. Everybody breathes. It is also extremely portable. We take it everywhere we go. So if you choose to practice with the breathing, it has the advantage of always being there. No matter how many times you forget it throughout the day, you can always take it up again. There's another in-breath. There's an out-breath.

Sometimes people think that when we speak of following the breath throughout the day, we are exaggerating for effect. We really can't mean such a thing. And maybe there is no one who can be mindful of every breath throughout the day. It is also true that there is a great deal of temperamental difference among practitioners. Some people who like to follow the breathing while sitting do not like to follow it in other postures, and that is all right. It is meant to be an aid to mindfulness, not an impediment. If you are better able to be mindful without it, fine.

Yet you really can't know until you make a sincere effort. One thing that many students find is that the more they pay attention to the breathing throughout the day—while eating, washing the dishes, listening to music, walking in the woods—the easier it is. The capacity to stay with the breath gets stronger and stronger, and the breath itself becomes more vivid and available and alive. It doesn't do much good for me to say that, of course. Really to discover it, you have to try it.

BRINGING PRACTICE INTO DAILY LIFE

My first teacher, J. Krishnamurti, clearly taught that life is the real teacher and our practice is every moment. I have never needed any convincing about that. I wasn't always as sold on using the breath throughout the day to help maintain wakefulness. But some years ago I studied the teachings of a Chinese master named Hsu Yun, who led retreats in which his monks used koans, and he encouraged them to keep the koan in mind throughout the day, from the time they got up in the morning until the moment they went to bed.

Later, I had access to some of his teaching from an earlier period, and he said the same thing about mantras: keep your mantra in mind throughout the day. That seemed a contradiction at first—should we be using koans or mantras?—but I eventually realized he wasn't emphasizing the method. Whatever your method, give yourself to it wholeheartedly. The more you use it, the more it will give back to you. Modern Westerners have not tended to use anapanasati in that way, but it can be done, to great benefit.

In the West, the teacher who has taught the most about using the breath in daily life is Thich Nhat Hanh. His books are full of practical suggestions. Buddhadasa spoke of daily life less. In order not to be overwhelming, I encourage beginning students to bring mindfulness at first to one routine activity per day. It can be anything: taking a shower, shaving, preparing breakfast, eating it (any meal that you consistently eat alone is a good one to practice with). As you give yourself over to this activity and feel the benefits of doing so, you'll be encouraged to bring mindfulness to other things.

The method is not to develop some kind of hyperattentiveness. It certainly isn't to bring greater strain to whatever you're doing. Actually, as it does in sitting practice, mindfulness should eliminate extra effort and make the activity easier. The idea is to bring a gentle attentiveness to whatever you are doing, to do that thing and nothing else.

One of the best ways to practice mindfulness is to see all the ways that you are not mindful, to see that while you're making the bed you're planning your day, thinking about something that happened yesterday, spacing out with a fantasy. As you would when you are sitting, just see that you have wandered away, and without blame, without condemning yourself in any way, come back to the activity of making the bed, with the breathing as a background if it helps you. Do that as many times as you need to, without worrying about how you're doing. Such awareness of unawareness will slowly bring about a change.

Sometimes students get confused about using the breath throughout the day. They give it an inordinate amount of attention, to the point that they are less attentive to the world around them. They're having a conversation with a friend and the person wonders if they're listening. "Well, not completely," they reply. "I was actually following my breathing." That isn't the idea at all. The breath is a gateway into the present moment, making our attention to it greater, not less.

There are times in the day when you can give almost exclusive attention to the breathing. You might be waiting for an elevator, waiting for a clerk to fill out a slip in a store, standing in line for a movie. For most people, these moments are dead time, when they become more distracted and less present. If you turn your attention to the breathing, even just for a few breaths, you can become more calm and centered. You are coming into touch with a kind of energy, and you emerge from the encounter refreshed.

Any number of moments that we normally see as inconveniences can be used this way. Thich Nhat Hanh speaks of the way stoplights can be like mindfulness bells in the monastery. In many places where Buddhism is practiced, and where people are working, a bell is periodically rung to bring people back to the present moment. The custom is to stop whatever you are doing for the space of three breaths in order to bring yourself back to the present.

People are often angry when they have to stop for a red light, overwrought and impatient. But it is possible to use red lights as occasions to come back to the breathing, get centered, and be refreshed (also to remind yourself not to be in such a hurry). You can use a ringing telephone the same way. Let it ring several times, and come back to the breathing. That will not only be a refreshing pause for you (so you're not always reacting frantically to outside stimuli, grabbing the phone as soon as it rings), but it will also enable you to be more present for the conversation you are about to have.

In my life around Cambridge and Boston, I frequently ride the subway. People carry on about how wearing such encounters with mass transit are and how depressing. But I often ride long distances and use these trips as occasions to meditate: no special clothes, no cushion, no bells or incense, just a guy sitting on the subway. I bring attention to the present experience and live those moments. It isn't depressing at all. Stretches of time that people typically hate—waits at the airport and at the dentist's office—can be used in the same way. There really isn't any time that needs to be dead. You can always bring life to it with awareness.

I love to walk for exercise, and I find my walks around the city to be wonderful occasions for mindfulness practice. All walking can be walking meditation. You can focus on your footsteps, on bodily awareness, or on the breathing itself, anything that brings you into the present. I frequently watch my mind during long walks (the ninth contemplation), which has always been one of my favorite practices. My collaborator in this book swims for exercise and finds that an excellent occasion for mindfulness practice. Any kind of physical activity—raking leaves, mowing the lawn—is ideal.

Of course, if I encounter a friend on my walk, that calls for a different kind of attention. Conversation is an intermediate activity, in which the main focus is on what the other person is saying, with the breath as a background to keep you from wandering away. Listening is an art in itself, often a lost art, as people space out or plan what they are going to say in reply. Real attention to what someone is saying is a great gift that can enliven a conversation and make it more meaningful.

I give many personal interviews, both on retreat and on a regular basis in Cambridge. These can be extremely intense encounters, as one person after another comes in to discuss some aspect of his or her practice. When the visitors are speaking, my focus is on what they are saying, on being open to them just as they are at that moment. The breathing in the background can be an aid to that, and between interviews I always come back to the breath, to refresh myself and be alert for the next person who is coming in.

There are moments in the day when it might be inappropriate to notice the breathing at all. If you are engaged in some extremely intricate task—brain surgery or root canal work or diamond cutting—the right thing might be just to give your full attention to it. That is mindfulness in that moment, to be fully with the task you are performing. If you see yourself wander away, come back. The principle isn't any different. You are just using the task as the object of focus instead of the breathing.

Finally the criterion is pragmatic. If breath awareness helps you stay attentive to the requirements of your situation, use it. If it doesn't, drop it.

TIPS FOR PRACTICING MINDFULNESS

At the center in Cambridge, I give my students a handout with the following reminders for practicing mindfulness throughout the day:

1. When possible, do just one thing at a time.

The famous advice of Zen is, "When you sit, just sit. When you walk, just walk. Don't wobble." It is always appropriate to ask yourself: What is my central action in this situation? If you are washing dishes, just wash. If you are driving, just drive. (That aspect of mindful living seems to be especially needed nowadays, as drivers roar by while they smoke a cigarette, drink coffee, listen to the radio, and talk on the car phone. Their bumpersticker says, "I'd rather be golfing." Sometimes you wonder who's at the wheel.) There might be a larger context in which the action is happening—someone speaking to you in the front seat—but generally, the primary activity is clear. Look into the present moment, see what that activity is, and do that.

It might be that the situation you're in is chaotic and confused. If it is, you need to be with the confusion, to take a good hard look at it, which might bring up some anxiety. But you have a better chance to come to clarity if you can allow uncertainty to be there, if you can resist the temptation to act just because you can't stand the uncertainty. Your own chaos can take you to clarity if you can experience it consciously. The breath can be helpful in that situation by acting as a brake on the mind's tendency to act impulsively, to prefer any course of action to the anguish that accompanies confusion. Sometimes wisdom is not to act.

People sometimes ask, How can I get anything done if I do only one thing at a time? Actually, we can be more effective. There is better attention and less tension when we do just one thing, and these factors more than balance the time that is saved by doing several things at once.

People also object that being strict about the one-thing-at-a-time rule will ruin their social life. I am not suggesting that you take your Thanksgiving dinner off to a corner of the room and focus on it exclusively. Large family dinners ask us to eat, drink, talk, and listen with the kind of panoramic attention which that kind of situation calls for. Samadhi in action needs to be both steady and pliable, moving from a focus on one person, or on one bite of food, to a wider focus, like a wide-angle lens that encompasses a number of people—less precise in detail but fully alive to the situation.

Most of our life, however, is not very complicated, or need not be, if we do just one thing at a time. The requirements of the situation are generally obvious and clear. Has your child just run into the house to tell you something? Listen!

2. Pay full attention to what you are doing.

We are paying full attention when there is nothing between us and the task at hand. If you are facing a sink full of dirty dishes and the mind is taken up with aversion to the task, impatience with how long it is taking, thinking about the movie you're going to see that night, you are separated from what you are doing. The hands are washing, but the mind is not. To be divided this way is to be less than fully alive.

Giving our whole body and mind over to a task, being undivided and intimate in our action, is what the Chinese masters called giving life to life. That can at times be a "doerless doing" as profound as enlightenment itself, the awakened mind in action. The capacity to bring our life into focus is available to us all the time, in situations both routine and dramatic.

The next time you do some simple task, see if extraneous thinking accompanies your action. That doesn't mean thinking is wrong, of course, just that it might not be helpful in that situation. If you're in a situation that requires thinking, just think! When you fill out your income tax form, just fill it out. Add your figures correctly.

3. When the mind wanders from what you are doing, bring it back.

Sometimes the mind wanders so much that you are no longer doing the task at all. At other times, the wandering is more subtle. In time, with practice, you can become much more sensitive to thinking and how it keeps you from being fully with an action. Don't try to be with the action in a muscular and willful way, just see the separation, and that seeing will restore wholeness to the action. Thinking is burned up in the flame of attention, and you are left just doing what you are doing.

4. Repeat step number three several billion times.

It is important to come back from your wandering gently and without blame. The practice is not just being with the object. It is seeing that you have wandered away, and coming back gracefully.

5. Investigate your distractions.

If the mind keeps wandering to something over and over, it might be helpful to take a look at what keeps coming up. It might be trying to tell you about something in your life that you need to do, or stop doing. Life has a way of breaking into our awareness when our response to it isn't adequate. When you switch to the distraction—assuming your situation is such that you can— make that your object of focus. Give some time to that, then return to your primary task.

The whole art of bringing the practice into daily life is learning to transfer the attention in that way. Do just one thing and do it fully, but be supple: if a child runs into the house screaming with a bloody knee, that replaces mopping the kitchen floor as your primary object. Give the child your full attention.

The art of mindful living requires keen interest and a lifetime of gentle and determined effort, falling asleep and remembering to wake up again and again. Too often meditators begin practice in a grim, joyless, and ambitious way, but that kind of practice—as the Chinese master Wu Men said—is "to wear chains and an iron yoke." Effort is needed to launch the art of mindful living, but not effort loaded down with comparison and self-condemnation. Mindfulness actually makes your mind lighter and freer.

Developing this kind of simplicity in your life does not limit you, as some people fear. It actually makes your life fuller. We have talked about the need to discover simplicity on the cushion, but it is just as necessary in daily life. We find real satisfaction not by the incessant longing after newer and newer goals but by taking joy in the small things that actually make up our lives.

My grandmother used to tell an old Jewish teaching story about that kind of joy. It concerned a man named Buncha Zweig. Buncha had been a good man, very kind and generous to everyone, had always worked hard and taken care of his family, and when he died he went to heaven. The angels met him on his arrival and said, "Congratulations, Buncha. You led a wonderful, virtuous life. Now you're in heaven and you can have anything you want. What would you like?"

Buncha pondered this question for a few moments, but couldn't think of anything.

"It's okay, Buncha," the angels said. "This is heaven. This is your reward for all those years of virtue, for always putting others before yourself. Just tell us what you want."

Buncha paused for quite a while this time, mulling over the question, but he still couldn't think of anything.

"Buncha, come on," the angels said. "This is paradise, already. The land of milk and honey. Everything a human being could possibly want is here, for the asking. You've got to be able to think of something."

Buncha sat for a while longer. Finally, he spoke. "All right," he said. "Do you think you could arrange for me to have a bagel and a cup of coffee every morning?"

BRINGING THE PRACTICE HOME

One of my hopes for this book is that, in addition to being a commentary on the *Anapanasati Sutra*, and thereby a means for meditators to deepen their practice, it will be an occasion for people new to the teaching to launch a practice. The sutra itself allows for such a hope. It starts with the most basic aspect of practice—following the in-and-out breath—and goes all the way to full liberation.

At the end of every retreat, I always try to give the new people a few tips for taking the practice back home. It is best to sit every day and to have a place in your house or apartment that is quiet and removed from activity that you can reliably use for that purpose. I can't really say how long your sitting periods should be. When I teach beginners, I start with periods of fifteen to twenty minutes and gradually work up to forty-five minutes and more.

On retreats, sittings run between thirty and sixty minutes—most are forty-five—and the regular sittings that we have here in Cambridge last for an hour. The amount of time is less important than the regularity. It is good to sit a little longer than you want to so you see the part of your mind that resists practice, but you don't want to torture yourself. In the same way, it is important to sit even on days when you don't feel like it. If you sit only when you want to, you will know only the mind that likes to sit.

I can't emphasize enough, however, how helpful it would be to find a teacher and a place to do intensive practice. People often ask me how they will know if a teacher is good, and it is hard to say; there is no mechanism for accreditation of Buddhist teachers in this country. You may be able to tell something from who that person's teachers have been and where he or she has studied. It is important to find a teacher who has been at the practice for a while, because long experience is what brings about real learning. Finally, you need to use the kind of discernment that you use in every other aspect of your life. If a person seems authentic and dedicated, start with him or her and see how it goes.

There are a number of meditation centers throughout the country, and a good way to find a teacher is to do a retreat at one of them. Often brochures will give descriptions of the teachers, and you can choose one who sounds like a good match for you. The kind of intensive practice that you do on retreat is extremely valuable and may be hard to do on your own.

Even if you live in a part of the country that is isolated from teachers and centers, regular trips to a center could, in effect, give you a teacher and a sangha (a group of practitioners). In ancient times, meditators often went off to practice by themselves for months at a time, traveling to see their teachers at regular intervals. Your practice could follow that model.

If you can't find a center, it is often helpful to start a sitting group on your own. Even if you can find only one other person who is interested, the two of you can get together once a week, do some sitting and walking meditation, perhaps listen to a tape by a teacher. It is extremely helpful to practice with other people. It gives support to your practice and helps you not to feel isolated. In time one other person might become two, then three. Substantial Buddhist centers have started in just that way.

It will also be a great help to your practice if you base it in an ethical standard of behavior. Buddhists for centuries have centered their practice on the precepts, often declaring themselves Buddhists in ceremonies in which they "take" the precepts, agreeing not to kill, not to take what is not given, not to misuse speech, not to misuse sexual energy, not to use intoxicants. The precepts require a certain amount of interpretation, of course, but really, they are a bare minimum for civilized living.

The precepts are not intended as externally imposed rules but as guides to mindful living. Our innate wisdom gradually sees that these are sane and intelligent ways to behave. Thich Nhat Hanh sees them as guides in the same way that the North Star is a guide for a navigator. We never quite reach them—no one practices right speech all the time—but they give us an indication of the direction we want to go. They are like warning signs, letting us know that these are areas of behavior where human beings get in trouble.

In traditional Buddhist training, there are three areas of practice, and they are often thought of as successive. Sila is ethical training. Samadhi is the development of a stable, calm, clear mind. And panna is the development of wisdom, what we have been referring to as vipassana. Instruction begins with ethical training, centered around the five precepts, moves on to meditation instruction, and then, finally, arrives at the wisdom that is its true goal.

But these three aspects of practice are not really successive and cannot be so neatly compartmentalized. In order to practice the ethical precepts at all, we need a certain amount of wisdom. We need to see, for instance—in our efforts to practice right speech—that wrong speech leads to suffering. Otherwise the precepts will have no real meaning.

It also takes a certain amount of mindfulness to practice the precepts. You have to be aware when you are speaking that every moment of conversation is an opportunity for right or wrong speech. People cause a great deal of suffering by things they say.

The breath can be a great help by giving you space around your words. Sometimes you are just moments from saying the wrong thing, but spending those moments with the breathing can give you the clarity to avoid it. In the same way, one of my students once told me of a situation in which he was perhaps thirty seconds away from committing a sexual indiscretion. He wanted to, and felt that the woman he was with did also. But in that brief period he was able to come to the breathing and bring himself back from a fantasy that had been very compelling. He had been carried away by a thought in the same way that he might have been on the cushion.

What he saw was that that sexual act would have violated a trust and caused him to be deceptive; it would very probably have hurt two families, his and that of the woman involved. In other words, he brought some wisdom to the situation. That is the kind of authority that the precepts can have, and it is the real reason for following them. You can save yourself from a lot of suffering.

There may be a time in our lives when we need to have rules imposed from the outside, but I have infinitely more confidence in a rule that is followed because a person sees the wisdom of it, because he or she has seen by looking into it that it is a good way to behave. The wisdom of the practice combines with the mindfulness we develop and eventually makes the precepts, not exactly unnecessary, just perfectly obvious. Why would you do something that is going to lead to suffering for you and the people you love? However, until authentic spiritual maturity develops— and for many of us it can take a while—it is extremely helpful to have the precepts as reminders.

It is also helpful for meditators to develop a healthy fear of situations that will bring suffering and a healthy shame for things they've done that they know are wrong. Either of those feelings can become excessive, obviously. But when we have done something wrong, and remorse comes up, it is helpful to experience it fully, to be intimate with it just like any other emotion. Fully experiencing it helps us avoid unwise action in the future.

Ultimately the practice is not divorced from any part of our lives. It is not some fetish or obsession with the breathing; it's about learning how to live. I often suggest that my students ask themselves the simple question: Do I know how to live? Do I know how to eat? How much to sleep? How to take care of my body? How to relate to other people? One of the most valuable— and simultaneously humiliating—moments in my life was when I realized that I didn't know how to live. I was a grown man with a Ph.D. and a professorship at a major university, but I didn't know how to live my life. So I set out to learn. I found that awareness can teach us everything we need to know.

It can be an especially valuable teacher in our relationships with other people. There is no area of human behavior that gets more attention nowadays, but much of it is the same old talk, the same tired thinking. Relationship is an extremely rich and viable part of practice, especially when you are able to use it as a mirror, so that you always see yourself in it.

Typically, we believe that other people make us angry, make us joyful or depressed. Buddhist psychology says simply: when A happens, B happens, which is different from saying that A causes B. When your partner does something and you become angry, you can see that as a valuable occasion for you to look at your anger, to bring your full attention to it. In time, as you keep bringing attention to a characteristic, it inevitably diminishes. Any relationship, even the most difficult one, can help you learn about yourself. And your learning is bound to affect the relationship.

The story is told that in one of G. I. Gurdjieff's communities, there was a man who was extremely obnoxious and was driving everybody crazy. Finally this person felt the hostility all around him, and left. But Gurdjieff chased after him and actually paid him to come back. He knew that the community could learn from that person in a way that they could from no one else. This isn't to say that you should stay year after year in a relationship that is hopeless or abusive. Obviously, wisdom would tell you to get out of such a situation. But it is to say that you don't need to tiptoe through life trying just to have "good" relationships.

One of my most vivid recollections from practice is when I was with my first Buddhist teacher, Soen Sunim, and he had decided to start a meditation center in New York. A group of us drove down with him in a car, and when we got to the place that he had picked out—a grim building on Fourteenth Street—we despaired. There were winos all around, drug users, drug pushers. It was exactly the kind of place we all would have run from on sight.

I will never forget his reaction. "No. Listen. A bad situation is a good situation." He knew that there was a lot of energy in that place, even if at first the energy seemed to be negative. And he did start a successful center there. That didn't mean he was blindly positive. On another occasion in another place, he tried to start a center, saw after a few weeks that it was located in the wrong place, and immediately—without regret or any sense of failure—closed it down. He was able to see situations clearly. But he didn't make snap judgments from surface appearances. He knew that there is much beneath the surface that we are not seeing.

SEAMLESS PRACTICE

I would like to end our discussion of daily life by talking about life on retreat. In other countries, Buddhist meditation is largely practiced by monks in monasteries, but in this country, for various reasons, meditation has been taken up in a major way by laypeople, who blend it in with the rest of their lives. It is a great help in that context. But it is also helpful—when you feel ready—to try a prolonged retreat.

I don't want to make exaggerated claims for retreats, but I do believe they deepen our practice as nothing else can. I lead many retreats as a teacher, but I also do a month-long self-retreat every year, and in the early years of my practice I did many long retreats as a meditator, not as a teacher. I found them to be invaluable, and many of the students whom I work with on a regular basis have found a way to make retreats a part of their lives.

Retreats can take a variety of forms. At our center in Cambridge, we have day-long sittings, weekend retreats, and—on long holiday weekends—three-day retreats. The Insight Meditation Society has some weekend retreats, but its most typical retreat, and the one I most often lead, lasts nine days. Meditators arrive on a Friday and leave a week from the following Sunday.

Full days at the retreat follow an invariable pattern. We rise early and have our first sitting at 5:45, followed by breakfast at 6:30 and a work period from 7:15 to 8:15. The morning is broken up into three periods of sitting and two of walking, as is the afternoon. In the evening there are two periods of sitting and one of walking, along with a Dharma talk. Aside from individual interviews with teachers every other day, retreats are conducted entirely in silence, with no eye contact and no communication by note. We also ask that meditators not read or write. We are offering nine days for practitioners to stay entirely within their own consciousness.

Other traditions may set up their days somewhat differently, but all of the Buddhist traditions that focus on meditation offer some form of prolonged retreat. Experienced meditators can do a three-month retreat at the Insight Meditation Society, and in some traditions retreats last for years.

Obviously, this is a special environment, much different from the lives most of us normally lead. Different styles of retreats have been intricately designed through the years—through the centuries, actually—to give practitioners a unique opportunity in which to look at themselves. And just as obviously, sitting seems to be the star of the show. What most meditators wonder the first time they come is how they're possibly going to be able to sit that much. It does take some getting used to.

Walking meditation, I suppose, is the costar, or has at least a strong supporting role. There are also the work periods, tasty vegetarian meals, and breaks, and the evening Dharma talk. But it is natural, especially for a beginner, to look at this schedule and think that sitting is what a retreat is all about. For many people, it is.

In addition to that dichotomy—sitting versus the rest of the day—students set up another one, thinking of retreats as intensive practice, and time away from retreats as daily life. As I've said, there are some people who find intensive practice very attractive, almost addictive. They look forward to retreats as the most wonderful part of life, and see daily life as a period to get through before the next retreat begins. It is the same as people on retreat who see sitting as the most important part, and are just passing time the rest of the day.

This dichotomy—which is definitely a false one—is one of the knottiest problems of Buddhist practice. If teachers emphasize the importance of sitting, students think that sitting is the essence of Buddhism. It is the real practice and produces all the great realizations. If, on the other hand, we emphasize daily life, people start to neglect sitting and think that all they need to do is fully live their lives.

What is really difficult about this whole matter is that there is truth on both sides. Sitting is special and very important to practice, as countless teachers have said through the ages. On the other hand, you can't exaggerate the importance of daily life.

But I believe that these dichotomies are themselves the problem. What is preferable is a seamless practice that doesn't see any one aspect of life as more important than any other. I find retreats a particularly good place to teach, but I do so by emphasizing— and at first this sounds like a paradox—daily life on retreat. Because I believe that, in a real sense, there is only daily life.

After all, even though you are on retreat, you still have to wake up in the morning, brush your teeth, take a shower, get dressed. You have to go to the bathroom at regular intervals. You have to eat meals. You still have a job to do, and sitting practice (though the relative amounts of time you do these things are reversed). It's very different from your usual life, and it also isn't. It's the same old stuff.

"At least we don't have relationships!" people on retreat often say. One impossible burden has been lifted. But that isn't really true either, though relationships are definitely different when you can't talk. Some of the meditators at the Insight Meditation Society have roommates, and others work with people on work teams. They are definitely relating to those people.

There is also the notorious "Dharma romance," in which meditators imagine a romantic relationship with someone else on retreat, only to realize, at some point, that it is all in their heads (and perhaps simultaneously realize that they have sometimes done the same thing out in the world). Some meditators work themselves into a frenzy because someone else was walking too slowly or wearing socks of different colors. So there may be no talking on retreat, but that doesn't mean there are no relationships.

I try to encourage meditators to see that there is daily life on retreat. Sitting is important, and walking is important, but so are meals and the breaks after meals. So is getting up in the morning and getting dressed. And so is the job that each meditator is assigned.

There are various ways of assigning these jobs. At some places where people do long-term practice, the teacher assigns the job as he or she gets to know the students. When I went to Korea, for instance, I was one of three Americans who were the first ever to practice Zen there. It was a big event, and people made quite a fuss over me, introducing me as a former professor and saying where I had taught. It was all quite impressive. So naturally, when it was time to give out the jobs, my teacher assigned me to the toilet.

It is also possible to let meditators pick their own jobs. That is what I used to do at IMS; people could pick work that was congenial to them. Someone who loved cooking could chop vegetables; those who liked to garden could work outside. I became aware in recent years that a fair number of veteran meditators were actually arriving hours early on the day that a retreat started, in the hope of getting their favorite jobs. Typically, an easy, enjoyable, and brief one.

I decided to change that procedure on recent retreats, having the jobs assigned entirely at random. There is a list of jobs, and meditators are assigned to them as they arrive, moving right down the line. People don't get to do their favorite jobs, or have any choice at all. They find out as they arrive what work they will do (though we do make exceptions for medical considerations).

I wasn't doing that just to be mean. I was trying to remove the feeling a retreat has of being an overly protected environment, where people control their destinies. After all, there are a hundred jobs on the list at IMS. Some are comparatively easy and rather enjoyable (chopping vegetables, dusting offices); others are not (cleaning bathrooms, scrubbing pots). Meditators who have hard jobs have been known to resent those with easy ones. Yet the emotions thereby aroused—anger, disgust, a feeling that life is unfair—tell us a great deal about ourselves and are ripe occasions for practice.

Insights don't come just when you are sitting on a cushion or doing formal walking meditation. When a contemplative is working, there are really two jobs. We're working on the vegetables or the toilet or whatever job we're doing. We're also working on ourselves.

So I encourage meditators on retreat to see it not as some specialized environment, where something extraordinary is going to happen, but as another form of life, just this moment followed by that one, no activity more important than any other. Our challenge is always the same, to be with each moment as it is. That will be true even if we become enlightened. How could it be any different?

Sometimes, in order to encourage that attitude, I use the metaphor of the breath itself. Really to inhale, you need to have exhaled, to get all the old air out of your system to make room for new air. In the same way, in order to inhale a new experience, you need to have exhaled the old one. Maybe it was wonderful (a sitting where you were still and quiet and felt a deep peace), or maybe it was dreadful (one where you were restless and experienced a lot of pain), but however it was, it is over, and it is time to walk or go to lunch. If that old experience lingers, it will color the new one. And you won't fully have the experience that is before you.

If meditators encounter a retreat that way, they are better able to enter into their lives after the retreat. It can be disconcerting, after nine days of silence, to find yourself suddenly in the midst of downtown Boston or the hubbub of Logan Airport. It might be natural to compare that to the idyllic environment you've just come from, or to see with dismay the disintegration of the hard-earned samadhi that you've developed over nine days. But you can't hold on to samadhi—you can't hold on to anything—and in any case that airport, or that raucous urban setting, is your life in that moment. Your task is to be awake to it. Only when the retreat is exhaled can the airport be fully inhaled.

We practice different forms—sitting, walking, retreats themselves—but before any form, before Buddhism or the Buddha—is life itself, waiting to be lived. Life is the real teacher, and the curriculum is all set up. The question is: are there any students? No form is unique, and on the other hand, every form is—sitting, walking, taking out the garbage, talking to a friend. Every form is unique, and so is every moment. When we see that, we are beginning really to practice.

7

Breathing into Silence

The teaching's voice is total silence, amid the
ringing wind chimes.

—Zen Master Hongzhi

VALUING SILENCE

At the heart of our practice, behind everything else, surrounding everything else, within everything else—such spatial metaphors are inevitably inadequate—is silence. We have little experience of silence in our world today, and the culture as a whole seems to value only more and more elaborate kinds of sound. Yet our sitting practice is silent, and retreats are profoundly so. Enlightenment has been called the great silence. In that way, Buddhist practice is at odds with the culture. It is at odds with every culture.

Most of us appreciate certain kinds of silence. We have all been in a room where the air conditioning is on, or a refrigerator is running, and it suddenly shuts off, and we breathe a sigh of relief. Parents of small children speak of the exquisite (and often short-lived) silence at the end of the day, with the children finally in bed, the television off, the house still. Some of us take vacations in quiet places, and even in our own houses we value moments when we can get off to a room by ourselves, to read a book or write a letter.

The silence I'm talking about is deeper than any of those and is sometimes—though not exclusively—reached in profound states of meditation. It extends all the way to the deepest stillness that human beings are capable of experiencing.

I became interested in introducing this subject into talks and practice groups several years ago. One reason was that I had a number of students who had progressed quite far in their meditation practice, had reached the threshold of a deep silence, but had encountered a profound fear and pulled back. With the goal of seeing students progress as far as they could, I asked myself how to deal with what was holding them back.

At roughly the same time, I saw an article in a newsmagazine about exploration of the oceans, saying that they were the last frontier left open to us. I couldn't help thinking there was one frontier the writer was ignoring: human consciousness.

We have explored certain parts of the mind, of course, and done intricate analyses of them. But there are vast realms that we have yet to touch, in all the millennia that human beings have been around. A few brave individuals have made inroads and have come back to tell us what they've seen. But most people don't even know these places exist. Meditators are psychonauts, to use Robert Thurman's term. We're explorers in the most fascinating realm of all.

For most people in the world today, life has much to do with verbalization. Talking. Reading. Writing. Thinking. Imagining. Language is a magnificent human invention (though other species seem to have done all right without it), but it is so embedded in our consciousness that we don't realize how much revolves around it. It wouldn't be too much to say that we worship language or that we're addicted to it. We equate it with living itself.

Another aspect of life for most people—related to language, obviously—is some form of action. Doing things. Creating. Moving things around, piling them up, arranging them. Engaging the body in physical activity, even just to enjoy ourselves in recreation.

184

In those two forms of endeavor, our culture—compared with others today, and especially compared with cultures from the past—is rich. We have more things, and more things to do, more varied uses of thought and language, than at any other time in human history. We're beyond rich. We're opulent.

Inwardly, however, we are paupers. Our throats are parched, and our spiritual bodies are gaunt. That is probably why we have so many outer things. We keep using them to satisfy a hunger that never gets any better. It seems insatiable.

We have a similarly vast craving for relationship. I know someone, for instance, with a great interest in mountain climbing who was recently extolling the wonders of the Internet. The night before, he had been talking to a fellow mountain climber in Siberia. That's wonderful, I said. But have you talked to your wife lately? Your children? We have this marvelous technology, but it doesn't seem to be helping with the life right in front of us. I have no doubt that if the Siberian mountain climber had showed up at my friend's door, he would have dialed 911. He wanted to know him on a screen, not face-to-face.

I don't mean to make light of our technology. The computer—like language—is a marvelous human invention. I'm writing this book on one. I have no doubt that the Internet is a wonderful resource, like having the greatest library in the world at your fingertips. But if accumulating information were going to save us, we'd have made it a long time ago.

The shortcomings of that kind of knowledge were brought home to me more than twenty years ago, when I was in Korea and studied with a monk named Byok Jo Sunim, one of the most memorable people I ever encountered. He almost visibly glowed, radiating the joy that the practice brought him. He was extremely loving, had a wonderful sense of humor. He was also completely illiterate. He couldn't sign his name.

While talking with him through an interpreter one day, I discovered that he thought the world was flat. I was absolutely astounded, and naturally decided to straighten him out. I went back to grade-school science, brought out all the classic arguments: if the world is flat, how can we sail around it? How come a ship doesn't just fall off the edge? He just laughed. He was adamant. I got nowhere.

Finally, he said, "Okay. Maybe you Westerners are right. I'm just an illiterate old man. The world is round, and you know that, and I'm too stupid to grasp it.

"But has knowing that made you any happier? Has it helped you solve your problems of living?"

It hadn't, as a matter of fact. It hadn't helped us with our problems at all. None of our knowledge had.

With all that we've learned, we human beings have not solved even the simple problem of living together. We have incredible technology, which can put us in touch with people on the other side of the world, but we don't know how to get along with the people in our own neighborhood, even in our own house.

One part of our culture is soaring, and another part is barely crawling. We are caught up in an illusion, a marvelous conjuring trick that has convinced us that the things we produce will make us happy. Not only are we the audience for this trick, we are also the magician. We have convinced ourselves.

We need to go much deeper into the mind. It's as if we are surrounded by vast fields, fertile soil as far as we can see, but we've only cultivated a tiny patch of it. We've done a wonderful job with that patch, but we need to explore the fields all around it. We need to get away from all the building and doing, coming and going, all the talking and thinking and reading and writing.

Silence is not a perfect word for what I'm trying to describe. There are no perfect words for it. In a sense I am using words to describe something that is the antithesis of speech (though it is also accurate to say that all speech comes out of it). Other teachers and other cultures have used words like *void* and *emptiness*, though those words have their own shortcomings.

Silence as I am using the term is a dimension of existence. You can live in it. It is what spiritual life is all about. It is quite literally unfathomable, limitless space permeated by a vast stillness. In a way it is inside us—that is where we seek it—though at some point in our exploration words like *inside* and *outside*, all the spatial terms I've been forced to use, don't mean a thing.

All of the accumulated history of human civilization— language, culture, thought, commerce—is relatively small compared with what is behind it. Silence is a dimension of existence, and for some people—throughout history, probably—it has been the primary dimension. They have been our most extraordinary individuals. They have learned to inhabit the world of silence, and to move out of it into the world of action.

You who are reading this book obviously have some interest in this dimension; otherwise you wouldn't have picked it up in the first place, and certainly wouldn't have gotten this far. And it isn't really that I am criticizing the other dimension of existence, the one we are all so familiar with, though it must sometimes sound that way.

My point is just that things have gotten out of balance. I have to sound critical just to let people know there is more to life than they have realized. We have such strong conditioning toward the world of thought and action that we need to weaken it, diminish its hold on us, before we can taste the vast richness of silence.

The first help I got in that direction was from my first Buddhist teacher, Zen Master Seung Sahn. He had come to this country from Korea and seemed to know only ten or fifteen English phrases when he got here. But he was extraordinarily skillful at using those phrases, a master of the Dharmic sound bite. He repaired washing machines for laundromats to support himself when he first arrived, and seemed to get by with just two phrases. "That broke? I fix." But before long he had a reputation as a Zen master, and on Friday nights as many as a hundred people, many of them university educated, would come to hear him give talks with those fifteen phrases.

In the tradition in which I now teach, interviews are quite informal, but in his Zen tradition they were formal, and every time

I came to him, no matter what I said, he always responded in the same way. "Too much thinking!" He would ring the bell, and I would have to leave. It was extremely humiliating. Finally one day I had a quiet sitting—given enough time, we all tap into silence—and came to him quite excited with the news. In that whole sitting, I told him, I had had only a few weak thoughts. He looked at me with utter disbelief. "What's wrong with thinking?" he said.

It isn't thinking that is the problem, he was letting me know. It is our misuse of it, our addiction to it.

Eventually I went with him to Korea for a year, and I vividly remember our flight over. I pulled out a sack of books, all my cherished Dharma books, which had been so important in leading me into the practice. "What's that?" he said. "Those are my books," I said. "Oh no," he said. "You don't read any books all this year." No books! All year! He didn't understand who he was saying this to. A Jewish intellectual junkie from Brooklyn.

"That's the whole problem," he said. "You know too much already. You merely know everything."

It was extremely difficult for me. I sometimes found myself reading the labels of ketchup bottles, I was so hungry for English words. But I followed his advice and didn't read a book all year. It was very liberating. Reading has been very different for me ever since, much lighter, with less attachment.

Similarly, when we have retreats at the Insight Meditation Society, we ask that meditators not read (even Buddhist texts), and not write (even a journal of their experiences). Eliminating these two activities is another way of diminishing the incessant hum of thought and language, of penetrating deeper into silence.

ENTERING THE ABODE OF SILENCE (-i's golden-)

Silence is extremely shy. It appears when it wants to and comes only to those who love it for itself. It doesn't respond to calculation, grasping, or demands; it won't respond if you have designs

(- or degrees)

on it or if there is something you want to do with it. It also doesn't respond to commands. You can no more command silence than you can command someone to love you.

There are concentration practices that achieve silence, but that silence is relatively coarse, willed, provisional, and brittle, very much subject to conditions. The silence I'm talking about is much deeper. It awaits us; it can't be grasped for. We don't create it; we find our way into it. But we have to approach it with gentleness, humility, and innocence.

The road to silence is filled with obstacles. The major obstacle is ignorance. We don't experience silence because we don't know it exists. And though I am emphasizing the difficulties, it is important to understand that silence is an accessible state for all human beings. It isn't just for hermits who live in caves in the heights of the Himalayas. It is available to everyone.

The first part of the journey is through the practice of breath awareness. Typically, when beginners sit down to follow the breathing, what they notice is a tremendous amount of noise, which seems pretty far from the exquisite stillness I'm talking about. The Tibetans have an expression for this stage of practice, "Attaining the cascading mind." That doesn't sound like much of an attainment. You notice that your mind is like a cascading waterfall, noisy and flowing all the time.

But the fact is that everyone's mind is like that, and most people don't know it. It is a major step to see that. Our world is very probably being run by people who don't realize their minds are like Grand Central Station at rush hour. Is it any wonder we're in the shape we're in and that things look and sound the way they do?

There is an old Jewish joke about a man who has gotten his hands on a beautiful piece of cloth and decides that he wants to make a suit out of it. He visits an expert tailor, who makes a number of measurements, says everything will be fine, and tells the man to come back in a couple of days. But when he returns, the tailor says, "No. I'm not done. Come back in a couple more days."

This happens four or five times, and the customer grows quite concerned, but finally one day he shows up and finds that the tailor has created an absolutely beautiful suit. "This is exquisite," the man says. "But do you realize that it took you longer to make this suit than it took God to create the world."

"Maybe so," the tailor said. "But you see my suit. Have you taken a look at the world lately?"

We don't wonder at the shape of the world once we see our cascading mind and realize that it is running the show. But there is no need to be impatient with it. Impatience doesn't help anyway. As you sit over a period of time and try to stay with the in-breath and out-breath, the mind will eventually quiet down, and you will notice moments when the breath is silky and soft and you are just with it. You may also notice the stillness of the pause between breaths.

That is a taste of silence, and you may find a certain refreshment even in that. It is an encounter with a very pure kind of energy. There is much more to come. But such early brief encounters give you faith to continue. And in dealing with silence, a certain amount of faith is extremely important.

Much deeper kinds of silence are available, but not through striving to attain them. Once you've achieved a certain calm with samatha practice, the way to silence is by making friends with your noise, really coming to know it. The biggest noisemaker is your ego, your tendency to attach to things as me or mine. The ego knows that there is no place for it in the world of silence, because silence belongs to no one. There will be nothing for it to appropriate. Silence is where the ego isn't.

In approaching deep silence, therefore, a much better approach—when you are ready for it—is choiceless awareness. A certain amount of silence is available through concentration, but a different quality of silence comes through understanding, which does not create silence but discovers what is already there. You are more likely to encounter such silence on a long retreat, when your mind has an extended period in which to slow down.

You sit with the breathing and allow everything to come and go, thoughts, feelings, sounds, sensations, mental and physical states. At first your attention will not be choiceless; you'll be directing it at this or that. But in time that tendency will fall away, even the breath won't be especially featured, and you'll be noticing whatever is, in an utterly undirected way, sitting with undivided presence in a state of total receptivity. You're not for or against anything that comes up; you just take a friendly, interested, accepting attitude toward it.

When the mind is allowed to roam freely in that way, it eventually gets tired of itself. It is, after all, just saying the same things again and again. It grows tired of all the noise and begins to settle down. As it does, you stand on the threshold of the vast world of silence.

Sometimes on retreats, meditators who have just been introduced to choiceless awareness will come to interviews and say, "Nothing's happening." We are so used to having things *happen* in our lives that we don't know the value of this nothing. But it is extremely valuable, the first step into the realm of silence. There is no need to do anything but just stay with it.

Another way to think of the approach to silence is that it grows out of true vipassana practice, centered on the thirteenth contemplation. You allow whatever arises to come into your mind, and what you see about all of it is that it is impermanent. In that seeing, there is a letting go and past that letting go is silence. From the clarity of a silent mind, one sees impermanence much more clearly. That clear seeing allows more letting go and a deeper penetration into silence. The two things feed on each other, what I'm calling wisdom and what I'm calling silence. Each deepens the other.

It is true that on the threshold of silence we often experience fear. It is the ego that is afraid. In the panoramic attention that you devote to choiceless awareness, the ego is not allowed to occupy center stage, where it thinks it belongs, and it begins to wonder what it will be like in silence, where it won't be present at all. This fear resembles the fear of death, because entering into silence is a temporary death for the ego. The great silence would be its permanent death. Naturally it is afraid.

When this fear comes up, it isn't an obstacle or hindrance. It is just one more aspect of the noise. Your encounter with that fear is very valuable, and the skill called for is just to stay with it. In time, like every other phenomenon, it will pass away. When it does, what is left is silence.

I have noticed in my own practice and teaching that the attainment of silence is somewhat related to the ability to handle loneliness, also to our acceptance of death. Especially for the ego, those things are closely related. We are afraid of being alone, and afraid to die, so we create company for ourselves with our thoughts, and they keep us from getting to silence.

It is therefore often helpful for a contemplative to do a certain amount of practice with death awareness. Apart from its inherent value, it helps us enter the realm of silence, which we fear because—like death—it is unknown. Actually, this realm is quite wonderful, an immense relief, but the mind doesn't know that. It might also be helpful, when a meditator feels ready, to go on prolonged self-retreats, where we may encounter loneliness in a profound way. Once we have made friends with our loneliness, silence will be much more accessible.

I might in this connection tell a rather personal story. My father died recently, after a long illness. We had been close all my life, and I had a great deal of grieving to do. At times I thought I was doing well with it, at other times not so well. I'm human, just like everyone, and not exempt from our tendencies to deny, repress, run away from, and intellectualize.

I took his ashes to Newburyport, Massachusetts, where I frequently do self-retreats, and floated them out to the Atlantic Ocean (which he loved) by way of the Parker River. Afterward I went to the house where I do my retreats. I had already sat with my grief a great deal, but at some level, apparently, I hadn't even begun, because that day I encountered more sorrow than I had thought was possible.

There had previously been elements of self-pity in my grieving, also elements of pity for my father. My self-centeredness was there, not allowing sorrow fully to flower. But now there was a direct experience of sorrow without any holding back, direct penetration of it for an extended period of time, real intimacy with it. Finally the sorrow ended. Beyond it was an immense silence.

I learned a great deal that day about the way that elements of the self keep us from fully feeling, and what is available to us if we let them go. Another term for such silence is absolute presence, which is only possible if there is absolute absence of the self.

Meditators often ask what to do when they get to silence. We typically have various agendas. Sometimes we are still basically afraid of it, want to taste it briefly and get out. Other times we sit in silence full of anticipation, waiting for something to happen. We view the silence as a door to something else. It is a door to the unconditioned, but if we attempt to use this door to get there, it stays shut.

If we are looking too hard for something special to happen, silence will collapse. We can also cause it to disappear by making it into a personal experience, naming it, weighing it, evaluating it, comparing it to other experiences we've had, wondering what we will tell our friends about it, or how we will shape it into a poem.

What we need to do instead is just surrender to it. Allow it to be there. It sounds like it must be just emptiness, a break from real living, but that is a failure of language. Silence is much more than that.

So what I advise meditators to do when they encounter silence is: absolutely nothing. Bathe in it. Let it work on you. The experience will make you realize what an inadequate word silence is for what I'm talking about. It is actually a highly charged state, full of life. It couldn't be more alive. The energy in it is subtle and refined but extremely powerful. It doesn't have to apologize to action.

Silence is also full of love and compassion. After you have been intimately embraced by silence, you come out feeling much more open to the world. You also come out—and this sounds strange, but it's true—more intelligent. You haven't acquired any information, of course. I'm speaking of another kind of intelligence, an intrinsic one. You're kinder, more sensitive, more compassionate. You can't achieve these things by trying, but if you value silence for itself, you will find them there.

SILENCE IN ACTION

Anyone who practices meditation has probably had some taste of silence. Maybe you've had ten seconds during a sitting when you were suddenly quiet and calm—you had no idea why—and you got up refreshed, infused with a new energy. Maybe you've come out of a sitting and noticed that the world looks different, or feels different, perhaps just for a little while. Meditators often report after a retreat that they feel more compassionate. They weren't trying to develop that quality; it just happened.

But the silence I'm talking about does not happen just on the cushion, and it is not something that you have to leave there. It is not actually damaged by noise. This is not the silence that is the opposite of noise. It is a quality that is intrinsic to us, an inexhaustible energy. It is not dependent on the approval of others, on what happens to us out in the world. It is not an experience that we have now and then. It is inherent fulfillment, which can permeate our lives. We can take it into the world and act from it.

Silence in action is the doerless doing that we've spoken of before, in which you *just* wash the dishes, just vacuum the floor. The ego is not present. Typically, whatever we do, we bring an "I" to it, attach to it as me or mine. But silence is the place where there is no ego, and silence in action involves acting in the world without making the action me or mine. In the process of uniting with the particular activity, we at least temporarily forget the self and are intimate with the vividness of what is there.

Various traditions come at this truth in different ways. In China, one answer to the question, What is enlightenment? was: Eating rice and drinking tea. Actually, you can eat and drink anything, but *just* eat and drink. The preoccupation with self goes into abeyance, and you are manifesting the depths of silence in the ordinary world. You can do the same thing with any action. That is what Zen means by No Mind, or Clear Mind. You step away from your past conditioning and are fresh, alive, and innocent in the moment.

Another answer to that age-old question is: The grass is green, the sky is blue. We all know that, of course, but when the mind comes out of the experience of being bathed in silence, it really sees it. It is an incomparable experience.

Early in my practice I had been sitting one afternoon in my apartment in Cambridge, then came out into the street and saw a Yellow Cab parked at the corner. I was waiting for a friend, in touch with my breathing, and focused on the cab. And I really saw it. I saw yellow. (I understood why they called it Yellow Cab.) It brought me to tears. In that state, anything could have had the same effect. A squashed beer can might have done it.

When the mind is clear of all obsession with me and mine, life is just there. Words can't describe it. It has an enormous impact on us, and we experience it much more deeply. Trying and striving do not get us to that point. An open clear seeing does.

So the point of all I'm saying is not to throw out culture, to abandon our involvement in the world. It is just to put things in better balance. I have not found any way to come into touch with silence except by going on extended retreats, with other meditators or by myself. I need a period without responsibilities in which the mind can exhaust its preoccupation with itself and settle into its inherent nature.

But I don't regard these retreats as the only worthwhile—or even the most worthwhile—moments in my life. That would reduce my life to just a month or so per year, or—even worse—to just a few moments of special insight. I have a very active life outside of retreats, and the key thing for me is to take what I learn on the cushion out into the world. The Dharma quest is to grow more and more into the large mind that leaves me and the story of my life behind. What is left is clarity.

We can't hanker after this state. We're all learning to be free, and the only way to do that is to see the ways in which we're enslaved. Occasionally we have big insights, but more often just small ones. Moments of self-preoccupation become moments of freedom when we see into and through them.

In some ways, all of these truths are expressed in one of the most famous stories in Buddhism, the meeting between Bodhidharma and the emperor Wu. Bodhidharma was a great Indian teacher and is credited with bringing Zen to China. The Chinese when he arrived had already been exposed to the doctrines of Buddhism and had done some remarkable things with them, but their interest was largely theoretical and scholarly. They were great with translations and commentaries, but no one was getting free. Bodhidharma, on the other hand, was a great master of the practice; following this encounter he would spend nine years in solitary sitting.

The emperor had been anxious to meet him, and immediately posed a question.

"I've contributed huge amounts of money for the building of temples, the financing of monks and nuns, the health of the sangha in general. How much merit do I get for all that?"

Bodhidharma could see that the emperor was speaking out of his attachment to me or mine. If he had done those things in another spirit, the results might have been different.

"No merit whatsoever," Bodhidharma said.

The emperor was stunned. He wasn't familiar with this kind of thinking (or nonthinking). He tried another approach.

"What can you tell me about the holy Dharma?" he said.

He was asking for Bodhidharma's exposition of Buddhist theory, a subject about which Chinese scholars could have gone on forever.

"Nothing holy," Bodhidharma said. "Just vast space."

This was a man who had spent some time in the abode of silence.

The emperor was exasperated. He was getting nowhere. He felt personally insulted.

"Who is it who is standing before me making these statements?" he said.

Bodhidharma looked him straight in the eye. "I have no idea," he said.

It is when we finally have no idea that we see things as they are.

Appendix

The Anapanasati Sutra

MINDFULNESS OF BREATHING

I have heard that on one occasion the Blessed One was staying at Savatthi in the Eastern Monastery, the palace of Migara's mother, together with many well-known elder disciples—with Ven. Sariputta, Ven. Maha Mogallana, Ven. Maha Kassapa, Ven. Maha Kaccayana, Ven. Maha Kotthita, Ven. Maha Kappina, Ven. Maha Cunda, Ven. Revata, Ven. Ananda, and other well-known elder disciples. On that occasion the elder monks were teaching and instructing. Some elder monks were teaching and instructing ten monks, some were teaching and instructing twenty monks, some were teaching and instructing thirty monks, some were teaching and instructing forty monks. The new monks, being taught and instructed by the elder monks, understood that which is lofty and excellent more than ever before.

Now on that occasion—the Uposatha day of the fifteenth, the full moon night of the Pavarana ceremony—the Blessed One was seated in the open air surrounded by the community of monks. Surveying the silent community of monks, he addressed them:

"Monks. I am content with this practice. I am content at heart with this practice. So arouse even more energy for attaining the unattained, reaching the unreached, realizing the unrealized. [To encourage your efforts,] I will remain right here at Savatthi [for another month] through the White Water-Lily Month, the fourth month of the rains."

The monks in the countryside heard, "The Blessed One, they say, will remain right there at Savatthi through the White Water-Lily Month, the fourth month of the rains." So they left for Savatthi to see the Blessed One.

Then the elder monks taught and instructed even more intensely.

Some elder monks were teaching and instructing ten monks, some were teaching and instructing twenty monks, some were teaching and instructing thirty monks, some were teaching and instructing forty monks. The new monks, being taught and instructed by the elder monks, understood that which is lofty and excellent more than ever before.

Now on that occasion—the Uposatha day of the fifteenth, the full moon night of the White Water-Lily Month, the fourth month of the rains—the Blessed One was seated in the open air surrounded by the community of monks. Surveying the silent community of monks, he addressed them.

"Monks, this assembly is free from idle chatter, devoid of idle chatter, and is established on pure heartwood: such is this community of monks, such is this assembly. The sort of assembly that is worthy of gifts, worthy of hospitality, worthy of offerings, worthy of respect, an incomparable field of merit for the world: such is this community of monks, such is this assembly. The sort of assembly to which a small gift, when given, becomes great, and a greater gift greater: such is this community of monks, such is that assembly. The sort of assembly that is rare to see in the world: such is this community of monks, such is this assembly—the sort of assembly that it would be worth walking great distances, taking along provisions, in order to come and observe.

"In this community of monks there are monks who have already realized the fruit of arahanthood,[1] destroyed every affliction, laid aside every burden, and attained right understanding and emancipation: such are the monks in this community of monks.

"In this community of monks there are monks who, with the total ending of the first set of five ropes of bondage, are due to be reborn [in the Pure Abodes], there to be totally unbound, never again to return from that world:[2] such are the monks in this community of monks.

---

1. In the Theravada tradition, arahants are those who have achieved the highest realization. They have rooted out all causes of affliction. They are no longer subject to the cycle of death and birth. They are no longer negligent in any way and have destroyed the ten fetters that shackle beings to the cycles of becoming: (1) self-identity views, (2) uncertainty about the path, (3) the superstitious use of rituals and practices, (4) lust, (5) hatred, (6) passion for fine material states, (7) passion for nonmaterial states, (8) conceit, (9) restlessness, (10) ignorance. In other words, arahants have realized perfect awakening.
2. This level of attainment is called *anagami*. Lust and hate don't arise in the

"In this community of monks there are monks who, with the total ending of [the first] three ropes of bondage, and with the attenuation of greed, aversion, and delusion, are once-returners who—on returning only one more time to this world—will make an end to suffering:[3] such are the monks in this community of monks.

"In this community of monks there are monks who, with the total ending of [the first] three ropes of bondage, are stream winners, steadfast, never again destined for states of woe, headed for self-awakening:[4] such are the monks in this community of monks.

"In this community of monks there are monks who remain devoted to the development of the Four Foundations of Mindfulness[5] . . . , the four right exertions[6] . . . , the four bases of success[7] . . . , the five faculties[8] . . . , the five strengths[9] . . . , the seven factors of awakening[10] . . . , the

---

mind of these meditators, and they have uprooted the five lower fetters. The remaining fetters keep them imprisoned to the conditions of living in the world.
3. This level of attainment is called *sakadagami*. These meditators have dropped the first three fetters and have weakened passion, aversion, and delusion.
4. Finally there is the *sotapanna*. These meditators have dropped the three lower fetters. They have entered the stream of awakening, which flows into the ocean of liberation in—at most—seven more lives.
5. The Four Foundations of Mindfulness—*satipatthana*—bring into focus the body, feelings, mental formations, and dharmas. They correspond to the four tetrads that compose the core of our practice with *anapanasati*.
6. In the four right exertions we arouse zeal and enthusiasm to (1) keep unskillful mental states from arising, (2) find a way to put an end to them if they have arisen, (3) cause skillful mental states to arise, (4) maintain and strengthen skillful mental states that already exist. Skillful mental states are those that benefit ourselves and others. Unskillful mental states do not; they cause suffering.
7. The four bases of success are qualities to be brought into proper balance so that meditation practice will succeed. They are (1) keen interest in doing the practice, (2) persistence in the practice, (3) intentness on the practice—wholeheartedness, (4) being discriminating in the practice, careful to see results of practice and make proper adjustments.
8. The five faculties are faith, persistence, mindfulness, concentration, and wisdom.
9. The five strengths parallel the five faculties and give us the capability to overcome the opposite of each of those qualities: lack of confidence, laziness, carelessness, distraction, and delusion.
10. The seven factors of awakening are mindfulness, investigation, persistence, rapture, serenity, concentration, and equanimity.

Noble Eightfold Path:[11] such are the monks in this community of monks.

"In this community of monks there are monks who remain devoted to the development of loving-kindness . . . , compassion . . . , appreciative joy . . . , equanimity[12] . . . , [the perception of the] parts [of the body][13] . . . , the perception of impermanence: such are the monks in this community of monks.

"In this community of monks there are monks who remain devoted to mindfulness of in-and-out breathing.

"Mindfulness of in-and-out breathing, when developed and pursued, is of great fruit, of great benefit. Mindfulness of in-and-out breathing, when developed and pursued, brings the four foundations of mindfulness to perfection. The Four Foundations of Mindfulness, when developed and pursued, bring the seven factors of awakening to their perfection. The seven factors of awakening, when developed and pursued, perfect clear insight and liberation."

MINDFULNESS OF IN-AND-OUT BREATHING

"Now how is mindfulness of in-and-out breathing developed and pursued so as to bring the Four Foundations of Mindfulness to their culmination?

"The meditator, having gone to the forest, to the shade of a tree, or to an empty building, sits down with legs folded crosswise, body held erect, and setting mindfulness to the fore. Always mindful, one breathes in; mindful, one breathes out."

---

11. The Noble Eightfold Path details the eight elements of correct practice: right understanding, right aspiration, right speech, right action, right livelihood, right effort, right mindfulness, and right concentration. Footnotes 5–11 are collectively called the Wings to Awakening and form the heart of the Buddha's teaching.

12. These four interrelated contemplations—loving-kindness, compassion, appreciative joy, and equanimity—are collectively referred to as the four *brahma viharas* or four boundless states of mind, because there is no limit to our mind when we are in these meditative states.

13. The perception of the parts of the body, sometimes referred to as reflecting on the unloveliness of the body, is used for counteracting excessive sexual lust or other attachments to the body as a self. The practice is to peer inside the body with the mind's eye, seeing the organs, the blood, phlegm, pus, urine, and so on. This practice can be a powerful antidote to the mind's tendency to glorify, romanticize, and identify with our image of the body.

THE SIXTEEN CONTEMPLATIONS

First Tetrad (Body Group)

1. While breathing in long, one knows: "I breathe in long." While breathing out long, one knows: "I breathe out long."
2. While breathing in short, one knows: "I breathe in short." While breathing out short, one knows: "I breathe out short."
3. One trains oneself:[14] "Sensitive to the whole body, I breathe in. Sensitive to the whole body, I breathe out."
4. One trains oneself: "Calming the whole body, I breathe in. Calming the whole body, I breathe out."

Second Tetrad (Feelings Group)

5. One trains oneself: "Sensitive to rapture, I breathe in. Sensitive to rapture, I breathe out."
6. One trains oneself: "Sensitive to pleasure, I breathe in. Sensitive to pleasure, I breathe out."
7. One trains oneself: "Sensitive to mental processes, I breathe in. Sensitive to mental processes, I breathe out."
8. One trains oneself: "Calming mental processes, I breathe in. Calming mental processes, I breathe out."

Third Tetrad (Mind Group)

9. One trains oneself: "Sensitive to the mind, I breathe in. Sensitive to the mind, I breathe out."
10. One trains oneself: "Gladdening the mind, I breathe in. Gladdening the mind, I breathe out."
11. One trains oneself: "Steadying the mind, I breathe in. Steadying the mind, I breathe out."
12. One trains oneself: "Liberating the mind, I breathe in. Liberating the mind, I breathe out."

---

14. Notice that the phrase "One trains oneself" appears here for the first time and continues for the rest of the contemplations. Training oneself implies a certain will and intentionality. The meditator lends some direction to the process, taking up the theme featured in each step and maintaining undivided attention to it. If the mind wanders, the meditator brings it back to that contemplation, so that the relevant lesson can be learned.

Fourth Tetrad (Wisdom Group)

13. One trains oneself: "Focusing on impermanence, I breathe in. Focusing on impermanence, I breathe out."

14. One trains oneself: "Focusing on fading away, I breathe in. Focusing on fading away, I breathe out."

15. One trains oneself: "Focusing on cessation, I breathe in. Focusing on cessation, I breathe out."

16. One trains oneself: "Focusing on relinquishment, I breathe in. Focusing on relinquishment, I breathe out."

THE FOUR FOUNDATIONS OF MINDFULNESS[15]

1. Now, on whatever occasion a meditator breathing in long discerns that he is breathing in long; or breathing out long, discerns he is breathing out long; or breathing in short, discerns that he is breathing in short; or breathing out short, discerns that he is breathing out short; trains himself to breathe in . . . and . . . out sensitive to the entire body; trains himself to breathe in . . . and . . . out calming the whole body: on that occasion the meditator remains focused on the body in and of itself—ardent, alert, and mindful—subduing greed and distress with reference to the world. I tell you, monks, that this—the in-and-out breath—is

---

15. My teaching of the *Anapanasati Sutra* emphasizes the sixteen contemplations to the point that, in abridging the sutra for inclusion in the text, I included only them. From a practical standpoint, the contemplations are all we need to launch the process of liberation. The sutra goes on here to discuss the four foundations of mindfulness and the seven factors of awakening. To comment on them adequately would require another book (and there are some fine books that have already done so, listed in the bibliography). But we have, in essence, already covered this material, from a slightly different angle and with somewhat different language. The most important thing to notice in the remainder of the sutra is that the Buddha is saying that both the four foundations and the seven factors develop out of the practice of anapanasati. This is in effect a ringing endorsement of the sixteen contemplations that we have gone over in so much detail.

Basically, the Four Foundations of Mindfulness are the tetrads that I discussed in the first four chapters of the book. As you move through the contemplations, you will develop the Four Foundations. That is what the Buddha is saying in this section of the sutra.

classed as a body among bodies, which is why the meditator on
that occasion remains focused on the body in and of itself—
ardent, alert, and mindful—putting aside greed and distress with
reference to the world.

2. On whatever occasion a meditator trains himself to breathe in
and out sensitive to rapture; trains himself to breathe in and out
sensitive to happiness; trains himself to breathe in and out sensitive to mental processes; trains himself to breathe in and out
calming mental processes: on that occasion the meditator remains
focused on feelings in and of themselves—ardent, alert, and
mindful—subduing greed and distress with reference to the
world. I tell you, monks, that this—close attention to in- and out-
breaths—is classed as a feeling among feelings, which is why the
monk on that occasion remains focused on feelings in and of
themselves—ardent, alert, and mindful—putting aside greed and
distress with reference to the world.

3. On whatever occasion a meditator trains himself to breathe in
and out sensitive to the mind; trains himself to breathe in and out
gladdening the mind; trains himself to breathe in and out steadying the mind; trains himself to breathe in and out liberating the
mind: on that occasion the meditator remains focused on the
mind in and of itself—ardent, alert, and mindful—subduing
greed and distress with reference to the world. I don't say that
there is mindfulness of in-and-out breathing in one of confused
mindfulness and no alertness, which is why the meditator on that
occasion remains focused on the mind in and of itself—ardent,
alert, and mindful—putting aside greed and distress with reference to the world.

4. On whatever occasion a meditator trains himself to breathe in
and out focusing on impermanence; trains himself to breathe in
and out focusing on fading away; trains himself to breathe in and
out focusing on cessation; trains himself to breathe in and out
focusing on relinquishment: on that occasion the meditator remains focused on mental qualities in and of themselves—ardent,
alert, and mindful—subduing greed and distress with reference
to the world. He who sees clearly with discernment the abandon-
ing of greed and distress is one who oversees with equanimity,

which is why the meditator on that occasion remains focused on mental qualities in and of themselves—ardent, alert, and mindful—putting aside greed and distress with reference to the world. "This is how mindfulness of in-and-out breathing is developed and pursued so as to bring the four foundations of mindfulness to their perfection.

THE SEVEN FACTORS OF AWAKENING[16]

"And how are the Four Foundations of Mindfulness developed and pursued so as to bring the seven factors of awakening to their perfection?

1. "On whatever occasion the meditator remains focused on the body in and of itself—ardent, alert, and mindful—putting aside greed and distress with reference to the world, on that occasion his mindfulness is steady and without lapse. When his mindfulness is steady and without lapse, then mindfulness[17] as a factor of awakening becomes aroused. He develops it, and for him it goes to the culmination of its development."

2. "Remaining mindful in this way, he examines, analyzes, and comes to a comprehension of that quality with discernment. When he remains mindful in this way, examining, analyzing, and coming to a comprehension of that quality with discernment, then investigation[18] as a factor of awakening becomes aroused.

---

16. The seven factors of awakening can be developed using any of the Four Foundations of Mindfulness; you can go through all seven while contemplating the body, then while contemplating feelings, and so on. The approach taken here doesn't get quite that systematic, but all seven factors are developed as you move through the sixteen contemplations of the sutra. Some of the seven factors—rapture and serenity—are spoken of quite specifically in the contemplations. In any case, the seven factors are another very skillful way to talk about the process that we discussed in the first four chapters of the text.

17. Mindfulness, of course, was one of the first subjects of our text, and we dealt with it quite thoroughly there. It is being developed as we focus exclusively on the breathing, or on any of the objects of the sixteen contemplations. As we practice with it throughout the sutra, it becomes more and more precise.

18. During the entire process of anapanasati we become increasingly sensitive to cause and effect. Early on, we might see how the breath is a powerful conditioner of the mind and body. In the fourth tetrad, we see the linkage between craving, attachment, and suffering in a clear way. When the Buddha talks about investigation, he is referring to that kind of seeing.

He develops it, and for him it goes to the culmination of its development."

3. "In one who examines, analyzes, and comes to a comprehension of that quality with discernment, unflagging persistence is aroused. When unflagging persistence is aroused in one who examines, analyzes, and comes to a comprehension of that quality with discernment, then persistence[19] as a factor of awakening becomes aroused. He develops it, and for him it goes to the culmination of its development."

4. "In one whose persistence is aroused, a rapture not-of-the-flesh arises. When a rapture not-of-the-flesh arises in one whose persistence is aroused, then rapture[20] as a factor of awakening becomes aroused. He develops it, and for him it goes to the culmination of its development."

5. "For one who is enraptured, the body grows calm and the mind grows calm. When the body and mind of an enraptured meditator grow calm, then serenity[21] as a factor of awakening becomes aroused. He develops it, and for him it goes to the culmination of its development."

Anytime we scrutinize some aspect of our experience, we are engaging in this quality of investigation and strengthening it. A mature vipassana meditator loves to investigate. It becomes natural and joyful to look with keen interest at any aspect of our personal experience. For meditation to become Insight meditation, it must include this factor of investigation, because it is careful examination of our experience—not to be confused with thinking about it—that brings insight.

19. Of course, we have needed persistence from the first moment that we attended to the breathing. But as mindfulness and analysis pick up momentum, they quite naturally give rise to much more energy to practice. This persistence is not stiff and tense but smooth and steady. It is the kind of effort that we use in a marathon rather than a sprint.

20. Rapture emerges out of persistence. It brings a contentment and lightheartedness to the practice, an open quality of mind that is more willing to receive every kind of situation with interest. When rapture becomes strong, it affects our entire energy system. Rapture emerges from the mind and has a powerful impact on the body, suffusing the whole being with joy.

21. Serenity develops as the rapture of the fourth factor smooths out into a kind of tranquillity. The ancients described rapture as the feeling that a parched man has when he discovers water in the desert. Serenity is the feeling of satisfaction he has after he has drunk the water. Serenity is calm but not dull; it is highly charged with life.

6. "For one who is at ease—his body calmed—the mind becomes concentrated. When the mind of one who is at ease—his body calmed—becomes concentrated, then concentration[22] as a factor of awakening becomes aroused. He develops it, and for him it goes to the culmination of its development."

7. "He oversees the mind thus concentrated with equanimity. When he oversees the mind thus concentrated with equanimity, equanimity[23] as a factor of awakening becomes aroused. He develops it, and for him it goes to the culmination of its development."

[Similarly with the other three frames of reference, feelings, mind, and mental qualities.]

"This is how the four foundations of mindfulness are developed and pursued so as to bring the seven factors of awakening to their culmination."

CLEAR KNOWING AND RELEASE

"And how are the seven factors of awakening developed and pursued so as to bring clear knowing and release to their culmination? There is the case where a meditator develops mindfulness as a factor of awakening dependent on seclusion . . . , fading away . . . , cessation, resulting in relinquishment.[24] He develops analysis of qualities as a factor of

---

22. Concentration develops out of serenity. Again, of course, we have been developing concentration throughout the practice. But it becomes much more powerful once a certain stillness is achieved.

23. Finally, when the process of anapanasati has really matured, we can contemplate everything with a clear, relaxed mind, one that can see anything that comes in front of it with unwavering attention. This is equanimity, the final factor of awakening.

24. We have been developing the Factors of Awakening from the moment we became mindful of our first breath. However, it is in contemplations fourteen through sixteen (fading away, cessation, and relinquishment) that the process gets intensified, to the point that these factors become genuine constituents of an awakening mind.

These final three contemplations are the stages where we can really come close to the mind's toxins of greed, hatred, and delusion and watch them be burned away by deeper and deeper seeing. The mind emptying itself of its poisons becomes the object of mindfulness, and all the factors of awakening are perfected. The Buddha saw this refinement of the seven factors as the last stage of practice. So whenever we refer to the fulfillment of the sixteen contempla-

awakening . . . , persistence as a factor of awakening . . . , rapture as a factor of awakening . . . , serenity as a factor of awakening . . . , concentration as a factor of awakening . . . , equanimity as a factor of awakening dependent on seclusion . . . , fading away . . . , cessation, resulting in relinquishment.

"This is how the seven factors of awakening, when developed and pursued, bring clear knowing and release to their culmination."

That is what the Blessed One said. Glad at heart, the monks delighted in the Blessed One's words.

---

tions of the sutra, we are referring to the Four Foundations and the Seven Factors as well.

Glossary

All terms are in Pali unless otherwise noted.

ANAPANASATI Mindfulness with breathing in and out. The meditation system taught by the Buddha in which conscious breathing is
used to develop both serenity and insight. The practice of *anapanasati*
is a natural progression of sixteen contemplations that fully explore
the mind-body process and lead to liberation.

ANICCA Impermanence, instability, flux, inconstancy. Conditioned
things are in ceaseless transformation: constantly arising, manifesting, and ending. Everything that is put together comes apart. Impermanence is the first of three aspects common to conditioned things.

ANATTA Not-self. The teaching that all things, without exception, are
not self; that they lack any essence or substance that could properly
be regarded as a "self." This teaching does not deny the existence of
things, but does deny that they can be owned or controlled or be an
owner or controller in any but a relative and conventional sense. *Anatta* is the third of three aspects common to all conditioned things and
is dependent upon ANICCA and DUKKHA.

ARAHANT A fully awakened being; a living being completely free of
all attachment to anything as being "me" or "mine." One who has
uprooted all KILESAS and experiences no more mental suffering. *Arahants* have attained the fourth and final stage of awakening.

BHIKKHU A male monk under the Buddha and up to the present day
who keeps the 227 monastic rules and lives dependent upon alms for
food. The term is sometimes used for any person who attempts to
develop skillful actions and abandon unskillful ones in order to realize liberation.

BUDDHO Awake, enlightened. An epithet for the Buddha, the one who
knows.

CITTA Mind-heart, consciousness. That which thinks, knows, and experiences. In a more limited sense, *citta* is what thinks, can be defiled by KILESAS, can be developed, and can realize NIRVANA.

DHARMA (Sanskrit; Pali: *Dhamma*) Truth, natural law, duty, order, "the way things are in and of themselves." *Dharma* is also used to refer to any doctrine that teaches such things. Thus the *Dharma* of the Buddha refers both to his teachings and to the direct experience of NIRVANA, the quality at which those teachings are aimed.

DUKKHA Unsatisfactoriness, suffering, pain; literally, "hard to endure, difficult to bear." *Dukkha* is the quality of experience that comes about when the mind is conditioned by ignorance into craving, attachment, egoism, and selfishness. It is the second characteristic of all conditioned things.

EKAGGATA One-pointedness of mind. The state in which the flow of mental energy is gathered together and focused on a single object.

GATHA Short Dharma verses that can be silently recited during daily activities to help one attend to the present moment.

JHANA The quality of mind able to stick to an object (e.g., a single sensation or mental notion) and observe it. The mental unification that comes about from such steady concentration results in total immersion in the object, as well as peace and happiness. There are eight levels of such absorption, each accompanied by an increasing degree of refinement.

KILESA A torment of mind. Craving, aversion, and delusion in their various forms, which include such things as greed, anger arrogance, envy, miserliness, dishonesty, violence, pride, conceit, and confusion.

NIRODHA Quenching, cessation. A synonym for NIRVANA, the end of attachment and DUKKHA. In the Buddha's teaching, *nirodha* always refers to the cessation of ignorance and clinging, not to the death of the person. It is the fifteenth contemplation of the *Anapanasati Sutra*.

NIRVANA (Skt.; Pali: *nibbana*) Liberation, the ultimate goal of Buddhist practice. *Nirvana* manifests fully when the fires of KILESA, attachment, and selfishness are completely and finally quenched.

NIVARANA The five hindrances that are obstacles to mental development: (1) craving for sensory gratification, (2) aversion, (3) sloth and torpor, (4) restlessness and agitation, (5) skeptical doubt.

PALI The canon of texts preserved by the Theravada school and, by extension, the language in which those texts are composed. The *anapanasati* discourse, the subject of this commentary, is one of these texts.

PANNA Wisdom, insight, discernment; correct understanding of the truth needed to quench DUKKHA.

PARIKAMMA Preparatory object for focusing attention when one starts to practice meditation. It would include such things as the repetition of the word BUDDHO ("the one who knows") to concentrate the mind. The silent repetition of the word is dropped once steadiness is attained. In the Thai forest tradition, BUDDHO is sometimes coordinated with the in- and out-breath to attain such a concentrated state.

PAVARANA The ceremony that concludes the annual rains residence, at which the BHIKKHUS invite each other to admonish them for their transgressions.

PITI Rapture, joy. Physical and mental lightness and agility resulting from purity of mind. It is the excited happiness of the fifth contemplation of the *Anapanasati Sutra.*

SAMADHI Concentration, collectedness, mental calmness, stability; the gathering together, focusing, and integration of the mental flow. Proper *samadhi* has the qualities of purity, clarity, stability, strength, and suppleness. It is perfected in EKAGGATA and JHANA. The supreme *samadhi* is one-pointed mind with nirvana as its sole object.

SAMATHA Serenity of mind due to concentration. *Samatha* practices lead to stillness of mind, but not to insight wisdom.

SANGHA The community of the Buddha's followers who practice thoroughly, directly, insightfully, and correctly. *Sangha* includes laywomen, laymen, nuns, and monks. The term is sometimes used more narrowly to designate only the community of monks, or of any people who have tasted some degree of awakening.

SATI Mindfulness.

SATIPANNA Mindfulness accompanied by discernment, common sense, insight wisdom.

SATIPATTHANA SUTRA The Buddha's discourse on the four foundations of mindfulness. It covers the four subjects for deep investigation: the body, the feelings, the mind, and the true nature of these formations. The *Anapanasati Sutra* uses conscious breathing to help accomplish the same objective.

SILA Morality; verbal and bodily action in accordance with the DHARMA. The essence of *sila* is nonharming of others and oneself. Laypeople use the five precepts as guides to such ethical conduct. They refrain from (1) taking life, (2) stealing (3) sexual misconduct (4) telling lies, (5) intoxicants and drugs that cloud the mind.

SUKHA Joy, happiness, bliss; literally, "easy to bear." *Sukha* is the subject of the sixth contemplation in the *Anapanasati Sutra*.

SUNNATA Emptiness. All things, without exception, are empty of "self" and "belonging to self." *Sunnata* is an inherent quality of everything. It also refers to the mind that is free of greed, anger, and delusion. NIRVANA is the "supreme emptiness."

SUTRA (Skt.; Pali: *sutta*) Discourse. The term is used in Theravada Buddhism for sermons attributed to the Buddha and certain of his disciples.

THERAVADA The "Teachings of the Elders." The only one of the early schools of Buddhism to have survived to the present day. Currently the dominant form of Buddhism in Thailand, Sri Lanka, Cambodia, and Burma.

VEDANA Feeling. The mental reaction to sense experience. There are three modes of feeling: pleasant, unpleasant, and neutral. *Vedana*, a mental factor, should not be confused with emotion, which is far more complex and involves thinking.

VICARA The aspect of concentration consisting of the mind's ability to sustain its contact and interest in the object.

VIPASSANA Insight, seeing clearly. The direct observation of mental and physical objects in their aspect of impermanence, unsatisfactoriness, and lack of an inherent, independent essence or self.

VIRAGA Fading away. The breaking up, dissolving, and disappearing of attachment; the subject of the fourteenth contemplation.

VITAKKA The aspect of concentration consisting of the mind's aiming toward establishing itself upon an object.

Bibliography

Bodhi, Bhikkhu, and Bhikkhu Nanamoli, trans. "Anapanasati Sutra: Mindfulness of Breathing." In *The Middle-Length Discourses of the Buddha*. Boston: Wisdom Publications, 1995.

Buddhadasa, Ajahn. *Anapanasati*. Translated by Nagasena Bhikkhu. Bangkok: Sublime Life Mission, 1980.

———. *Mindfulness with Breathing*. Translated by Santikaro Bhikkhu, Boston: Wisdom Publications, 1997.

Buddhaghosa, Bhadantacariya. "Mindfulness of Breathing." In *The Path of Purification*. Kandy, Sri Lanka: Buddhist Publication Society, 1979.

Fuang, Ajahn. "Breathing." In *Awareness Itself*. Valley Center, Calif.: Metta Forest Monastery, 1993.

Gunaratana, Bhante. *Mindfulness in Plain English*. Boston: Wisdom Publications, 1993.

Hart, William. "The Training of Concentration." In *vipassana Meditation as Taught by S. N. Goenka*. New York: HarperCollins, 1987.

Kamalashila. "Mindfulness of Breathing." In *Meditation*. Glasgow: Windhorse Publications, 1992.

Lee, Ajahn. "Beginning Concentration" and "The Basics of Breathing." In *The Skill of Release*. Valley Center, California: Metta Forest Monastery, 1995.

———. "Quiet Breathing." In *Food for Thought*. Translated by Thanissaro Bhikku. Valley Center, Calif.: Metta Forest Monastery, 1989.

Maha Boowa, Ajahn. "The Tracks of the Ox." In *Things as they Are*. Translated by Thanissaro Bhikkhu. Udorn Thani, Thailand: Wat Pa Baan Taad, 1988.

Nanamoli Thera. *Mindfulness of Breathing*. Kandy, Sri Lanka: Buddhist Publication Society, 1982.

Nanamoli, Bhikkhu. "Treatise on Breathing." In *The Path of Discrimination*. London: Pali Text Society, 1982.

Nanayon, Upasika Kee. "Every In- and Out-Breath" and "Breath Meditation Condensed." In *An Unentangled Knowing*. Translated by Thanissaro Bhikkhu. Kandy, Sri Lanka: Buddhist Publication Society, 1996.

Nhat Hanh, Thich. *Breathe! You Are Alive*, revised edition. Berkeley, Calif.: Parallax Press, 1996.

———. *The Blooming of a Lotus*. Boston: Beacon Press, 1993.

———. *The Miracle of Mindfulness*. Boston: Beacon Press, 1987.

Nyamgal Rinpoche. *The Breath of Awakening*. Kinmont, Ontario: Bodhi Publishing, 1992.

Nyanaponika Thera. "Mindfulness of Breathing." In *The Heart of Buddhist Meditation*. York Beach, Maine: Samuel Weiser, 1993.

Sumedho, Ajahn. "Mindfulness of the Breath." *The Mind and the Way*. Boston: Wisdom Publications, 1995

———. "Only One Breath." In *The Way It Is*. Hertfordshire, England: Amaravati Publications, 1991.

———. "Watching the Breath." In *Mindfulness: The Path to the Deathless*. Hertfordshire, England: Amaravati Publications, 1987.

Suzuki, Shunryu. "Breathing." In *Zen Mind, Beginner's Mind*. New York: Weatherhill, 1970.

Thanissaro Bhikku. *The Wings to Awakening*. Barre, Mass.: Barre Center for Buddhist Studies, 1996.

Vimalaramsi, Ven. U. *The Anapanasati Sutta*. Kelong, Malaysia, 1997.

Webu Sayadaw. "Dhamma Discourse III." *In Selected Discourses of Webu Sayadaw*. Wiltshire, England, 1992.

Woodward, F. L., trans. "Kindred Sayings about In-Breathing and Out-Breathing." In *The Book of the Kindred Sayings*. London: Pali Text Society, 1979.

Resources

For further information regarding Insight Meditation, please contact one of the following practice centers.

Abhayagiri Monastery
16201 Tomki Rd.
Redwood Valley, CA 95470
(707) 485-1630

Barre Center for
Buddhist Studies
149 Lockwood Rd.
Barre, MA 01005
(508) 355-2347

Bhavana Society
Rt. 1, Box 218-3
High View, WV 26808
(304) 856-2111

Cambridge Insight
Meditation Center
331 Broadway
Cambridge, MA 02139
(617) 441-9038

Insight Meditation Society
1230 Pleasant St.
Barre, MA 01005
(508) 355-4646

Metta Forest Monastery
P. O. Box 1419
Valley Center, CA 92082
(619) 988-3474

Spirit Rock Meditation Center
P.O. Box 909
5000 Sir Francis Drake Blvd.
Woodacre, CA 94973
(415) 488-0164

Audio tapes of talks by Larry Rosenberg and other Insight Meditation teachers are available from:

Dharma Seed Tape Library
Box 66
Wendell Depot, MA 01380
(508) 544-8912